GOLD DUST ON SUNBEAMS

An Anthology of Poems

By

Avantika Vijay Singh

Qurate
quratebooks.com

Gold Dust on Sunbeams
Avantika Vijay Singh

Published in 2025

© Published by

Qurate Books Pvt. Ltd.
Goa 403523, India
www.quratebooks.com
Tel: 1800-210-6527, Email: info@quratebooks.com

ISBN: 978-93-58987-27-0

FOREWORD

By Santosh Bakaya

This collection of 78 poems, penned by the versatile Avantika Vijay Singh has a shimmering title, ***Gold Dust on Sunbeams***. It alludes to the ephemeral nature of life, like dust floating in time's vastness, and yet, shimmering like gold when illuminated by life. This dust is beautiful, not unlike the golden dust sparkling in sunbeams, providing a natural pathway of light, hope, and renewal.

In the section, **The Temple of Twilight**, her words mesmerise and bewitch and it appears as though she has got hold of a golden pen which gives the readers glimpses into the golden grandeur of the glowing sun, its rising and setting splendour in Kashi, Sundarbans, Goa, Kashmir, and near Jaipur! How smoothly the words flow from her elegant pen! What a dreamlike ambience she conjures with her pen! What mystique! What enigma! What sublimity!

She captures well the sacred grandeur of the Shankaracharya Temple and the philosophy of dissolution in Advaita Vedanta in sublime poetry,

"the temple, in splendour stands, silhouetted in greys
of the magnificence of its crossways,
with the *lingam* in its sanctum—
the formless in His iconic form...
where the finite
meets the infinite...
... in the sweeping splendour
of the Zabarwan range spread in languor,
swooping on the surface of the Dal Lake,
I dissolve in surrender to the landscape—" [*A Morning at Shankaracharya Temple*]

Cosmic unity, a recurrent theme, is echoed in this prayer,

"And, when the time comes
May I gently dissolve
Into the universe,
Merging with the elements—
Gold dust on sunbeams,
Dancing in the golden sunshine—
A part of the eternal landscape." [*A Prayer to Sunset*]

And, yet in humility, she adds,

"I, too, am cosmic dust...
Let me, too, scatter light,
in the inky darkness.
Let the golden light illumine my mind,
turning my dust to shimmering gold." [*A Prayer to Sunrise*]

In nature, she finds an antidote to everything that is despairing and dismal and makes her burst forth in happy songs. As she starts humming, the reader also joins this song, which slowly becomes a chorus of hope.

"Nature, the theatre real
where happens magic surreal.
Nature, the temple of hope
where dawns strength to row life's boat.
Nature, the cure
that heals souls for sure." [*Temple of Hope*]

Cosmic Dance has poems where Singh fluidly weaves physics with metaphysics, science with mythology, and spirituality with poetic finesse in seamless harmony.

"in the space of mass, energy, and time,
the universe dances to its silent rhythm...
every atom and sub-atom sways and shifts,

changing shape and form in time's mists…
in *Ananda Tandava*—the dance of bliss" [*Lord of Dance*]

One can sing paeans to this profound life if we acknowledge its shortness. In the section, **Float Free**, the poet visualizes herself as the object of the moment, floating free in the universe. Her poems have the magical power to cleanse our cluttered souls of anguish and anxiety. What a liberating feeling it is to find her becoming a dust mote, whispering:

"I am the mote of dust floating on the golden sunbeam.
I am the dust that pervades the outer reaches of space
And the inner reaches of the earth.
I am that mote of dust swirling sometimes in the darkness,
And at other times floating on sunbeams.
In my being, I carry experiences over time...
Some good, some bad…
Let go, let go...
Lighten your burdens
And float free and light." [*Float Free – Mote of Dust*]

We watch awed, as she transforms into a butterfly,

"flying in the breeze,
towards light,
towards freedom,
towards liberation.
Freed from the paralysis
that holds my body
in captivity," [*Float Free – A Butterfly*]

Before we can blink an eye, she is a dandelion floating free with,

"No sense of
Self-aggrandisement
Self-entitlement
Arrogance

Hubris
Anger—

Float free
Free in the golden sunshine
Free on the breeze
Free in my being
Free in the universe of love." [*Float Free – A Dandelion*]

As we read on, we see her becoming a snowflake, a raindrop, an egret, floating free, cruising unshackled. She becomes a snowflake, whose form is determined by the coldness of the Atmosphere.

"Form that is at one with the universe
Universe that takes my journey to the womb of the earth
Earth that absorbs me gently when I fall
Fall I, with grace when I drift
Drift I in peace with the universe." [*Float Free – A Snowflake*]

"Floating free in the universe
A raindrop am I
Free…free…free…
Drifting with the winds
Knowing no beginning
No end.
Landing on a leaf here
A flower there
An eave or an awning
I care not for the landing…
There I stay curled
For time infinitesimal
Reflecting the beauty of creation.
And, then I roll off
Pulled by the forces of nature
To submerge into creation
From whence I came." [*Float Free – A Raindrop*]

In **Quilling for Humanity**, we hear nature talking to us in sublime tones, spreading the message of peace far and wide, and, before we know it, we are vibrating rhythmically to nature's melody, all our senses alive and alert. With the poet, we yearn that every shackled human being is set free, and dreaming unfettered dreams.

In *Within and Without*, she is alive to the sounds of nature:

"I close my eyes
My ears open...
My senses alive to the chirp of the birds
Cheep cheep, hoo-po hoo-po, piao piao
The birds' calls transmit
Vibrations of *shanti,* peace, bliss...

I am a blissful being
At peace with nature
At peace with myself...
A continuation of nature as
My being vibrates in rhythm"

In another powerful poem, *Awaken the Goddess Within,* she appeals to all to,

"Awaken the Goddess within
irrespective of gender; Awaken
devotion, austerity, resplendence, creation.
Destroy the darkness of negativity
borne from the ego, like the Mahisasurmardini.
Awaken the divine feminine
And bring peace and harmony to the world!"

And we say Amen to that.

In the section **Being Woman,** she once again excels. In *Set Me Free*, she beseeches the world,

"Tie me not in chains of gold
for my worth is manifold.
My golden anklets moor me
to a cage with no key.

Set me free,
and let me be...
an uncaged bird
with dreams unfettered.

I am not anyone's chattel
to be levied with taxes in battle.
I am a human, too, with potential
not merely a womb to populate exponential.

Tie me not
into youthful matrimony's knots.
Give me a chance...
in the golden skies to dance.

Set me free,
and let me be...
an uncaged bird
with dreams unfettered."

In the **Pandorathon**, a word marathon run annually by The Significant League, she is at the wittiest and creative best, writing on whimsical prompts, which she calls, "more delicious than croissants." Writing on such quirky prompts was definitely not an easy task, but she does it with elan making use of beautiful imagery and metaphors. She once again does an exquisite job, writing on prompts given during CePoWriMoWE by poets in the group, WE Literary Community, run by another powerful poet, Smeetha Bhoumik.

Authentic, captivating, and inspirational, her poems shine like gold dust, filling us with sparkling hope. Invisible and reassuring hands suddenly appear, and hold us. Thus, is born a peaceful, harmonious, song where there is no self-aggrandizement, no hubris, and an unwavering faith in rejuvenation and revival. This student of nature has given us life lessons in simple, effective words but which have a great impact. Like the sun rays, that she so lovingly talks of, her poems leave a golden trail in their wake, brightening the deep crevices of the mind, removing the dismal darkness and despair, filling them with the soothing sounds of nature, the hoopoe's calming call, and the fragrance of flowers.

Let me conclude by reproducing a stanza from her poem, *Altar of Hope:*

"Good will be the future...
Future like gold dust on sunbeams,
Sunbeams that stream silently
Silently streaming from the sun
Sun that never wavers in its faith to shine"

This is a book that should adorn every nature lover's bookshelf, and also the bookshelf of every lover of good poetry.

Here is wishing Avantika Vijay Singh all the best for her future literary endeavours.

Avantika Singh, let me borrow a few words from you and say, may you

"*Shine, shine, and let your hope shine...
Shine like gold dust,
Gold dust on sunbeams.*"

Santosh Bakaya, PhD

Poet, novelist, creative writing mentor, essayist, academician, columnist, and TEDx speaker, internationally acclaimed for her more than thirty books written across myriad genres.

PREFACE AND ACKNOWLEDGMENT

This book is a collection of 78 poems entitled *Gold Dust on Sunbeams,* dedicated to my mother, Mrs Anita Vijay Singh, on her 78th birthday. The title refers to the ephemeral nature of life, like dust floating in time's vastness, and yet, shimmering like gold when illuminated by life, providing a natural pathway of light, hope, and renewal. The book explores themes of nature, spirituality, impermanence, transformation, human resilience, interconnectedness, gender, and social justice.

Temple of Twilight has poems of a meditative quality on both dawn and dusk born from sublime experiences at various places. They form a sacred geography for me where time and space dissolve in the dance of the spirit with nature, reinforcing my faith that being in harmony with nature is the best way of experiencing divinity. Nature inspires... and I respond with my own odyssey.

Cosmic Dance explores and celebrates the infinitesimal yet radiant nature of existence, weaving physics with metaphysics, portraying existence as stardust, and contemplating upon the cosmic order, transcendence, and impermanence.

Float Free explores poems where I imagined myself as an object of the moment, floating free in the universe. In these moments of zero gravity, dawned quiet truths—freedom from hubris, ego, or aggrandisement. Perhaps, shed of these burdens, they fly or float light.

Quilling for Humanity is born from prompts in anthologies, festivals, or writing marathons where poets dream of a world adorned with love, compassion, hope, and respect. I, too, dream of a world beyond the darkness and despair... a place where sunbeams pierce through the shadows offering hope and gold dust dances, as we dwell in interconnectedness and oneness, recognising the dignity and divinity in all. This section includes the poem "*Within and Without*" for which I received the Certificate of Excellence 2024 for the *Ratna Tripathi Memorial Award* from the Asian Literary Society (ALS).

Being Woman includes a few poems on empowerment, both as a passionate declaration of agency and a need for social change. It also celebrates women through tributes to those who inspired me to write for prompts or otherwise. Many poems in this section are written to prompts given in Celebrate Poetry Writing Month with WE (CePoWriMoWe) in April 2024, run by the Women Empowered (WE) Community, founded and powered by a powerful poet, Smeetha Bhoumik. A few poems, written for CePoWriMoWe, have also been included in the previous section, where they fit thematically and are noted. Participating for the first time in CePoWriMoWe was a rewarding experience, culminating in my receiving the *WE Gifted Awards 2024 for Tributes*. So, thanks, Smeetha Bhoumik for creating this space.

Pandorathon includes a few poems from the Pandorathon, a word marathon run annually by The Significant League (TSL), a virtual poetry group on Facebook, founded by Dr Ampat Koshy. In 2024, the prompts were posted daily by Dr Santosh Bakaya, based on which poems were written. Dr Bakaya's prompts are unique, quirky, and often quaint, and range from the whimsical to deeply emotional with an almost magical quality. As a result, one has to dive deep within oneself to mine untold stories outside the normative experience of life. And, I shall always remain grateful to this master storyteller for allowing us to explore and embrace our emotions, enabling me to write poetry that brings a deeper meaning to both writing and life.

Many of the poems here have been published in various anthologies and journals, nationally and internationally. I am grateful to the *Setu Bilingual Journal, The Wise Owl |The Daily Verse, Destiny Poets International, Yugen Quest Review, Lotloherian, Borderless, Literary Vibes*, and *Free Voice* for publishing my poems.

Some of my poems have been featured in anthologies by the Soul Scribers Society, and I am deeply grateful to Geethanjali Dilip, Curator of the *Yercaud Poetry Festival (YPF)*, for her thoughtfully chosen poetic themes and for entrusting me to edit the anthologies. At one of these festivals, on the silver shores of Puducherry, I had the privilege of meeting Gayatri Majumdar, the Curator of the *Puducherry Literature Festival*. When I requested her to write the Afterword, she graciously agreed. I remain eternally grateful for her thoughtful and eloquent words, which capture the essence of my poetry—its deep-rooted connection with spirituality and my journey as a poet. Meeting her in Auroville was serendipitous, and I cherish our shared connection.

I am deeply humbled and immensely grateful to Dr Santosh Bakaya for her luminous Foreword, which beautifully captures the book's essence with the gold of her warmth and poetic grace. My heartful thanks to Satbir Chadha Ma'am and Dr Koshy, for their generous words that adorn the back cover of this book and to Geethanjali for her very incisive and precise Critical Review. I cannot thank them enough for their generosity, love, and praise. I feel truly blessed to have my poetry read and written about by people of such immense literary stature. I am immensely grateful to the community of poets and friends whose encouragement motivates us to write more.

My immense gratitude to Sujeet Shyam, the God of design, for crafting the cover and the artwork on the section dividers with such artistic prowess. A heartfelt thanks to *Qurate Publications* and Mr. Rama Harmalkar—a gentleman who keeps his word—for bringing this book to life.

My heartfelt gratitude to God and Swami Chidrupanand*ji,* Head of Chinmaya Mission, Noida, for guiding me in my on-going journey of understanding Advait Vedanta. I remain deeply beholden to my family for their unwavering love and support, especially my husband, Sanjay, and Romsha—my go-to people—for anchoring me while my mind floats in the world of words. I am immensely thankful to my parents for reading each of my poems, encouraging me, and showering me with their love and blessings. And to my in-laws and brother, Vikas, for their unassuming presence and support.

And, a heartfelt thanks to you, dear Reader, for reading my book.

Avantika Vijay Singh

Contents

FLOAT FREE

QUILLING FOR HUMANITY

BEING WOMAN

PANDORATHON

temple of twilight

Prayer to Sunrise

Let the future dawn,
golden like the sun,
travelling unseen through
the inky, icy, darkness
of the universe,
without revealing itself.
But when it enters
the Earth's atmosphere,
dust scatters light,
radiance washes over the world...

I, too, am cosmic dust...
Let me, too, scatter light,
in the inky darkness.
Let the golden light illumine my mind,
turning my dust to shimmering gold.
Let the golden light pass through my being,
flowing boundless,
melting the frost of boundaries,
indifference and despair,
seeding roots of love
for flowers of joy to bloom.

O, Lord! Grant me the strength,
to be the dust that scatters the light.
Grant me the wisdom to turn my life of dust
into a shower of gold, scattered on the wind...
gold dust on sunbeams...

A Morning in Pondicherry

on the silver beaches of Pondicherry, I stand,
my toes dipping in the sand,
looking at the vast ocean—
the universe in harmonic motion,
crimson shimmers on the silver horizon,
swirling in silver clouds this season,
silver waves dance in the sea,
specked with white in the breeze,
silver within me swirls—
silver waves of ecstasy...

in the dawning emerges a yawning,
my companions and I feel the pull
and no longer can we simply stand,
silent witnesses to that majestic spectacle—
the sun rising in grandeur in the sky's womb,
speckling the waters in splendour—
within us stirs a call to be a part of that dawn...
we walk barefoot, shoes in hand
towards the lighthouse grand,
drawn towards it like ships of yore
that must have landed on these very shores...

not wanting this morning ever to fade,
another beach we visit, the Promenade—
giant black rocks rim the beachfront,
guarding from the current,
their precious pearls—
the colonial buildings in pastels,
whispers of an age gone by,
their louvered windows breathing air,
seeing images from time rare—
my eye struggles to fit in my mind's eye,
the legacy of history besides
the ocean's vast mystery...

on one wall is a big, butterfly painted,
we flit to it, and stand between its wings
to float free in time,
the ocean air beneath our wings…
we go to those black rocks we saw earlier,
warm from seeing nature's magnificence daily,
absorbed in their being the glory,
and there in companionable silence
we stand, watching the sunrise,
between currents of time and tide…

on silver beaches, I see the 'golden light'—
the *brahman* within me stirs,
my life spirit, from my body, ascends
vapourises... drawn to the heavens,
upwards and outwards it reaches
dancing on the beaches…
I merge into the dawning,
filling my yawning—
a grand celebration
of all that is within and without…

Sunrise Near Jaipur

from the ruins near Charan Mandir,
a temple dedicated to Lord Krishna,
on the way to Nahargarh Fort,
I watched the sunrise framed in time—
a study in contrasts—

there stood the ruins that had seen many a sunrise,
had known the valour of *rajahs* past,
outlasting them all,
yet crumbling to nature's quiet presence,
its stone bricks teetering and falling…

and there stood the inky horizon,
filling gradually with a golden glow
embracing us all...
the waters below, reddening
with the light of the awakening.

in Charan Mandir, in the midst of Ambika forest,
Lord Krishna's *charan* (feet) for eternity rest…
the forest still flutters to His flute's whispers,
peacocks, in timeless grace, quiver and dance,
shedding their feathers in devotional shivers…

and there we stood in the liminal space,
fleeting shadows like dust in time…
faith behind us, the dawn ahead,
watching the sunrise,
my daughter—Romsha, my friend—Parul,
and I—totally mesmerised…

at that moment precisely,
a bird alighted on a branch
silhouetted in the sea of dawn's gold—

Sunrise in Kashi

under the dawning skies, on a boat I sail
in Kashi, where thinnest is the veil,
between the worlds—physical and metaphysical—
time and space dissolve in the city mystical...
the rivers of my mind merge and flow
in eternal consciousness with the river's sun-lit glow,

on the flowing waters
time shimmers gold, flowing by on time's altars—
history unfurling, the morning light revealing...
forts, palaces, *ashrams*, and temples sparkling,
on *ghats* supine like the cosmic man's spine,
built for their proximity to the sacred design

dawn touches the city from time's dawn
from Lord Shiva's infinite column of light drawn—
light that pierced the three worlds (*trilok*),
manifesting as the *jyotirlinga* bespoke—
dawn bathes the buildings and temples
along the *ghats* in colours transcendental...

colours from them run into the river
rippling like brush strokes of a painter...
colours flow on the banks like art
colours flow right into my heart...
soft images come into focus
on the dreamlike tableau before us

In the liminal space I stand
between what was and what is
echoes of time on waters linger
sifting truths on reflections that glimmer...
vaporising illusions that fade like smoke
from the funeral pyres that nothingness evoke...

A Dawn in Mysore

on a January morning in Mysore
my spirits soar,
from my hotel room I see
Vrindavan Garden in all its mystery…
cloaked in silver mists
shimmering silver in the gossamer rain
adorned festively in flowers, fine…

I walk across the gardens,
imprints my footsteps leave
on the dew-drenched grass…
my eyes mesmerised, my ears alive
to the music of water drops
those tiny, tiny silver droplets
from the fountains sprinkling
in a continuous stream tinkling
in evanescent time—

deep amidst the bougainvillea blooms,
bathed in the cascading waters of a fountain,
hidden from common view,
I come upon the bust of Lord Shiva's statue…
and stand transfixed
for there I see betwixt
His matted locks…
those very tiny, silver drops
that mesmerised me so—

drops flowing gently in eternal time
dissolving in the sea of cosmic consciousness

An Invocation to Sunrise

May the sun rise
in the depths of my mind—
A sunburst with multiple rays,
a multi-pointed star,
bursting through silver-lined dark clouds,
cutting through space and water,
leaving a golden trail
in its wake.

Let the sun's rays fall
upon the wavering slopes of my mind,
lighting the deep crevices within
where dwell darkness, despair, and doubt.
Let them dispel the tenebrosity and turmoil,
awakening my mind to the light
of changeless consciousness
where flowers of hope bloom.

And when the sun rises,
let the waters of my mind
be calm and tranquil,
lit golden by the rising sun,
with lotuses blooming.
Let my life, too, shimmer gold
in the awakening—
gold dust on sunbeams…

A Morning at Shankaracharya Temple

while the rest of India was sweltering,
this morning, in Kashmir, was drizzling...
a soft grey, in May
and that's how began the day—

past the Dal Lake, we sped by,
which upon the morning seemed to sigh,
stirred by its tryst
with the breeze in the silver mist

we crossed the check post in time
and climbed the verdant hills sublime...
and then began the sheer climb...
steep, grey steps that each must take in their time

we slowly climbed, paused, and rested...
for the steep steps, our resilience tested,
then climbed again
till at last we saw the shrine main—

an imposing structure cobbled in grey
that you can only fully see from the crossway—

the temple, in splendour stands, silhouetted in greys
of the magnificence of its crossways,
with the *lingam* in its sanctum—
the formless in His iconic form...
where the finite
meets the infinite...
... in the sweeping splendour
of the Zabarwan range spread in languor,
swooping on the surface of the Dal Lake,
I dissolve in surrender to the landscape—

a crossway of sorts,
a confluence in time of thoughts
for here did Shankracharya*ji* meditate
and carried forth the word of the Advait,
and to these harmonies, the air still vibrates...
a cosmic crossing, the *brahman* merging...
... and I becoming...
Aham Brahmasmi...

The Call of the Light

Soft shimmering sunshine
dancing in woods divine—
streaming from the heavens
enthralling the senses,
gold dust gleaming on greens—
hope floating on sunbeams.

Hope, rising with the sun,
in glimmering gold spun...
Darkness dies and decays
as with light, hope rises.
In the temple of dawn,
light, my spirits adorn.

Arise from the slumber...
see the sublime wonder.
Sating of the senses
can only yield darkness.
Arise! Awaken to light
to become the light.

Listen to the call of the light,
surrender to its might,
to guide you right...
Connect to the divine,
through nature's mighty shrine—
Unity, the ultimate design!

Note: Published in *Destiny Poets International* on 5 January 2025.

Temple of Hope

Nature, the theatre real
where happens magic surreal.
Nature, the temple of hope
where dawns strength to row life's boat.
Nature, the cure
that heals souls for sure.

The chirping of the crickets
matched the twinkling of stars in the thickets.
The calming call of the Hoopoe bird
hoo-poo-hoo-poo-poo I heard
under the canopy of stars
that soothed my heart with its gentle powers.

And then gently blushed the horizon
as though shyly waking heaven,
lifting the violet veil
for the sun to sail.
And the light shined forth
illuminating the world with its birth.

The branches bursting with blooms
to my lips bring happy tunes.
The fragrance of the flowers...
The chatter of the mind overpowers.
No anxiety, no depression, no stress
do I in their presence possess.

Seeing a boy with earphones I wondered...
Could the music that in his head thundered
ever match the Hoopoe's calming call?
Oh! When will those earphones fall?
When will he know the transcendence,
for which nature offers cues in abundance?

Note: Published in *Literary Vibes – Edition CXLIX* (31 January 2025)

A Sunset in Kashmir

a sunset I wanted to see
and my darling father obliged me...
but never in my wildest dreams did I imagine
the fire of passion
that lit up the skies
in the sun's daily good-byes,

but more of that later
for the journey was equally major,
not something in your backyard
but in nature's own backyard—
travelling miles and miles
into virgin mountainside that smiles,
bedecked in white summer flowers...
the evening ephemeral, as the fragrance of their showers...

we reached high up—a Land's End—that none can surpass
on a road that allowed only one vehicle to pass,
unfolding our shaken limbs from those jouncing roads
we stretch and stretch... my imagination explodes...
our country's majestic flag proudly flutters in the breeze,
embracing the valley of Kashmir that I see
laid out whole like a bowl, with the Jhelum,
a silver ribbon awash in twilight's hues,
looping and turning, slowly meandering through...

the great dog, the men's guardian against the bears nearby
jumped high in delight, looking for a friendly pat,
I wondered how my father had all those years
served the nation on frozen frontiers,
just like these men did now—
my respect grew for all those who don the olive green,
fearlessly forging into the unforeseen...
the roses, growing in the wild beside me,
I offer to all in time—past and present, in my mind's eye...

I lifted my eyes to the heavens...
and saw them blooming in the red of those very roses
that bloomed all over the mountainside...
the Jhelum, too, shimmered crimson in their glow,
as though all of creation, was in that moment, aglow...
then how could we not be?
we stood in hushed reverence
with nature in silent communion,
a part of that eternal landscape...

as night yawned, the stars filled the sky
and to everyone we bid goodbye...
I wondered if the evening could be any more sublime
but the way back felt equally lost in time,
into the dark we travelled alone
where just the light from our jeep shone
taking us into a world that seemed unreal
showing sights, surreal ...

a bear meandering into the jungle
like the meandering Jhelum...
a fox suddenly emerging and then disappearing
in the magical light as I struggled to find my mooring,
crowned by a porcupine standing with its quills wide open
quivering in its dance of existence in the hush unspoken
and there danced my soul
in the dance of creation whole...

Sunset Over the Koel

somewhere in Jharkhand,
ahead of Palamu perhaps
rest sal and deodar forests eternal,
and there flows the Koel...
murmuring stories immemorial
in its journey to the sea

astounded I am, by the rich red,
raw beauty of the Palash...
its flowers, bold and unapologetic
like women who have grown into their own,
women confident of themselves...
they may not be graduates
but with wisdom they brim,
rising with a sense of agency,
defying gendered expectations
that fractured society—
perhaps lit by the embers of rebellion
that their blood carries...

it's close to the hour of sunset,
we rush towards the Koel
for perennial seekers we are...
and those very colours of the Palash
I see the sky wear—
honouring the land, it journeys over,
not to be outdone, the river too resonates
resplendent in crimson hues...

softly, softly... blows the wind...
like the whisper of the Mahua
that gently sways on the breeze,
the sun grows soft, loses its fire,
fulfilled with the exhilaration
of having played its swan song,

and now ready to fade into
the gentle stillness,
into the flowing waters of the Koel,
like the Mahua meets her destiny ethereal...

and I am lost in this grand play
that I see at *godhuli*...
much like the cattle returning home
surrounded in the play of dust,
their bells tinkling in the twilight,
those very bells tinkle in my ears
looking at the sunset over the Koel...

A Sunset in the Sundarbans

on the tide we cruise,
in a motorised barge, looking for views
of the sunset in the river…
how wrong I could be—you must consider,
for a sunset is not something to see
but something to feel, to touch free
and to revel in the wonder
as the fragile fabric of your being is torn asunder...

the crimson sun sinks rapidly into the river
setting hearts in symphony to quiver,
but darkness does not immediately follow…
instead, remains a reddish orange glow—
like the embers from a dying fire
softly glowing, suffusing into my soul's fibre—
and into this soft saffron glow,
the motorised barge climbs slow…

the tide flows high, like my emotions,
bobbing on time's oceans
and I am suffused in that glow
as waves of bliss grow…
in eternal time, I dissolve and flow,
at one with the rippling river
which now within me flows
sat-chit-anand…

A Sunset in Goa

Years later, as I reflect,
on the beauty of a Goa sunset...
In a wash of fiery scarlet and molten gold
the waves whisper secrets old.

The sunset melting into the ocean
creates a giant canvas of connection...
Larger than their individual realms,
is their combined beauty that overwhelms.

The moment divine and heartfelt,
when two worlds melt...
A dance of colours meets the heart
as the sun and sea embrace, otherwise light years apart.

Who is the creator
and who the creation
becomes the question
as the sun merges with its reflection.

Such beauty resides
when worlds melt on the ebb and flow of tides.
To melt is divine,
for in it rests creation's potential to shine.

Note: Published in *Destiny Poets International* on 19 February 2025 under the title 'A Melting Sunset.' It was also among the 'Highly Commended' poems of the month.

A Prayer to Sunset

I pray to thee,
Let my setting years be,
A walk in the river of sunset...
With the golden glow ahead of me,
And the flowers of my life spread behind me...
Each flower iridescent,
In the radiance of the golden glow!

In the canopy of His shade,
May I find rest
And the flowers I have sowed,
Dazzle and stretch
Into lands infertile.
May the winds carry their fragrance
Far and wide.

I pray to thee,
May the sea winds blow kindly
In the winter of my life,
Enfolding me in the golden glow
Of the resplendent setting sun,
Warming my old bones
And giving life to my breath!

May my footprints on the golden sand
Find home for the crabs to burrow
In the shifting sands of time,
And survive
When the waves crash
Upon the shores
In their might.

And, when the time comes
May I gently dissolve
Into the Universe,

Merging with the elements—
Gold dust on sunbeams,
Dancing in the golden sunshine—
A part of the eternal landscape.

Note: Published in *Destiny Poets International* on 19 July 2024 and also included in the category of 'Highly Commended Poems' for the month.

cosmic dance

Lord of Dance

in the space of mass, energy, and time,
the universe dances to its silent rhythm…
every atom and sub-atom sways and shifts,
changing shape and form in time's mists…
in *Ananda Tandava*—the dance of bliss

a dance of creation and destruction,
the pulse of all matter and existence—
particles popping in and out of existence
in rapid fluctuation…
Shiva's cosmic rhythm

the landscape of reality
an ever-changing dynamic illusion...
shifting and swaying
to His *damaru*
in the dance of creation and destruction

the world, a transient place
and I, a sentient being in contemplation,
seeking liberation…
from ignorance and illusion
that the Lord personifies with one foot raised high

the other foot planted firmly
on the back of ego/ignorance
crushing sorrow…
surrendering to the divine
paving the way for the awakening

in the silent rhythm of His dance,
where forms constantly shift on reality's expanse
I am a fleeting quark in consciousness' streams

glowing briefly like gold dust on sunbeams…
surrendering to Shiva's dance in the visible universe

Note: Published in YQR 2025

Dance of Light and Shadows

in the dance of the seasons,
as the sun transitions
from *Dakshinayana* (southern hemisphere)
to *Uttarayana* (northern hemisphere),
Bhishma's crossing comes to mind—
resting upon a bed of arrows lined,
awaiting the cosmic gateway to liberation
with the north wind's elevation,
following the path of light
where the soul rests bright...

moksha...

freedom from ties to earth,
freedom from the cycle of birth and death,
Om Shanti, Shanti, Shanti...

moksha...

disillusion of illusion
with deep self-realisation...
of one's true nature in time and space—
attained by Lord Shiva's grace,
the keeper of time himself
Mahākāla—
eternal, luminous, floating free
Aham Brahmasami...

Joyous Dance of Life

In time…
People go away,
shedding their mortal coil.

A lifetime lived like
a glorious grain of sand
on the vast beach of life,
whipped to life
by the breath of the wind
and dancing there ecstatically,
the dance of life!

When the wind stops to rest
from its ecstatic frenzy,
it comes to rest again
at one with the beach,
in the vastness of time,
space and energy,
to be swept away by the waves,
perhaps deposited on other shores.

And, then one day again
when the wind plays hard,
the grain of sand rises once again
to dance its euphoric dance of life,
perhaps on those very shores
or even distant ones
for it is its nature
to rest and dance,
dance and rest!

But until it rises again,
all that remains is
golden memories—

gold dust on sunbeams—
rising from the sands of time
to joyously, gracefully
dance its golden dance,
swirling to the lilting tunes of the wind
whirling like a dervish on the beach.

Gold dust on sunbeams
floating in the sunshine...
Warming the heart
with the warmth of memories.
A smile here, a laugh there...
Some heartwarming words
and the warmth of actions past,
warming the heart
like golden sunshine on a winter morning.

Note: Published by *Setu Bilingual Journal*, November 2023

Sparkling, Shimmering…

Sublime is life,
Life is sublime,
Exploding like fireworks
On the night of *Amavasya*
Sparkling, shimmering…
Shimmering, sparkling…

Rising from the firmament,
Brilliant forms impermanent.
Lighting the darkness,
Bursting into a thousand stars,
Sparkling, shimmering...
Shimmering, sparkling…

Drawing oohs and aahs
From the enraptured onlookers,
Staring at the symphony
In the theatre of the night,
Sparkling, shimmering...
Shimmering, sparkling…

Mirroring the astral symphony
On a smaller timescale,
Such is life
In the vastness of the universe
Sparkling, shimmering...
Shimmering, sparkling…

Live it, live it…
Light up the night
Be the celestial symphony
Dancing in the universe's magnitude
Sparkling, shimmering…
Shimmering, sparkling…

Note: Published in *Destiny Poets International* on 23 September 2023

Ganpati Bappa

He came,
He sat,
He saw,
He lived amongst us...
I didn't want to send him off,
But I did
Because in sending him
I release my
Attachment,
Greed,
Ego...
I let go...
For there is nothing
Permanent.

The next day…
I wake up in the morning
To see nothingness…
Just flowers floating free
At the site of *Visarjan*
And the words of a famous Vedic *mantra*
Slip automatically
"Om purnamadah purnamidam purnat purnamudachyate
purnasya purnamadaya purnamevavashisyate
Om Shaantih Shaantih Shaantih."

A powerful reminder—
Everything emerges
From the infinite Universe
And again, merges back with it.
The void is not nothingness
But wholeness…
An optical illusion
For the Universe is whole, and
"From wholeness comes wholeness."

Note: Published in *Literary Vibes – Edition CXLV* (27 September 2024)

Child of the Earth

iridescent hues of silver and slate
crowd the darkening horizon in veined agate,
swirling ominously in the pewter skies,
rumbling their disenchantment to give up the prize—
prized cargo of precious water,

precious water, life-giving water that flows,
no boundaries, no constrictions, knows...
but flows freely in gay abandonment
with the spirit of life abundant,
to the rhythm of the falling rain,

the falling rain that rises and falls,
in wanderlust to shores that enthrall
rising from the earth to the silver skies,
beckoning the wanderer with their promise, wise
that everything comes full circle…

full circle of life, take I
for a child of the earth am I,
rising from the temporal dust,
roaming the transcendental skies hushed,
sometimes falling into cycles of hope and dismay…

but the Lord reminds to seek liberation
from this eternal cycle of aspiration,
pewter skies or falling rain
are one and the same—
dissolution of the illusion of opposites…

Shiva, the Aghori, with ash on his face
and Shiva, the Shankara, bestowing wisdom and grace
not dual extremes, but of cosmic flow, one stream
where merge fear and grace…
destruction and creation...
life and death…

The Dance of Healing

Ecstatic is the river,
that to glorious heights rises,
dancing wild in torrents of silver,
through valleys and mountains, it slices.

But in its long course to the sea,
in the sands, it often stutters, running dry—

Life is not much different—
ecstatic are we with our glories
till one day… the river is no longer magnificent,
running dry in the sands of loss or injuries.

Alone in the universe of grief,
we suffer for the loss of flow we once knew,
mired in frustration from the lack of relief
wondering when life will renew,
cursing the turns taken wrong in misplaced belief.

Know that healing is not a return,
where the goal is as before—the same,
but a transforming on a new turn,
to something greater… a brighter flame.

Much like the Lord's Tandava; cosmic energy
pulsating to His *damru's* cadence.
His flowing locks in frenzy
tossing and turning the plane of existence
unravelling the old, familiar reverie—
tempests carrying away the resistance.

Shiva dancing in cosmic glory,
the dance of creation and destruction—
the ending is not merely an ending
but a pause, an interlude in the symphony

before the leap to the transition—
burning the old, the known... the rudimentary.

Fall away... habits, people, relationships...
the stage set for the next step of evolution...

On to this levelled plane
flows the Ganga from His matted locks
nourishing, life-giving like the rain
seeding creation again...
the river of life halted by insurmountable rocks
flows once again.

Healing is to dance again like the river,
rising from the razed rage of the Tandav's passing,
accepting the vulnerabilities that make us quiver,
but transforming suffering into a new beginning...
Just like the Lord, who drank the *halahala*,
transformed suffering into saving creation.

Healing is showering the Ganga of patience, love, and care,
not giving in to despair...
He, the Lord of Healing, blessing the essential repair—
not just merely returning to living, but rising 'aware'
a renewal that the Lord symbolises... a 'new' beginning—
gold dust on sunbeams shimmering...

float free

Float Free – Mote of Dust

I am the mote of dust floating on the golden sunbeam.
I am the dust that pervades the outer reaches of space
And the inner reaches of the earth.
I am that mote of dust swirling sometimes in the darkness,
And at other times floating on sunbeams.

In my being, I carry experiences over time...
Some good, some bad...
They have their own power to throb and haunt.
But am I just a victim of those circumstances?
Why then should I give them more power
To hurt me, haunt me?

Rise, rise above the circumstances
Let go of the experiences from your mind
That twist and turn your soul like molten steel
And drive you into the deepest darkness.
Seek the light and float free!
Let go, let go...
Lighten your burdens
And float free and light.

Note: Published by *Yugen Quest Review*, 24 August 2023

Float Free – A Butterfly

A butterfly am I,
flying in the breeze,
towards the light,
towards freedom,
towards liberation.

Freed from the paralysis
that holds my body
in captivity,
my mind floats free
like a butterfly,
on the breeze.

Where my body cannot go,
goes my mind.
I feel every undulation
as I float free
on the wind,
visiting flower to flower.

Freed from the
dark recesses of my mind
that hold me in the abyss of a cocoon,
I float free
like a butterfly,
on the golden sunshine.

Awakening my inner Athena,
my mind floats free
in the golden sunshine,
going where my body cannot go…
A butterfly am I…
Floating on the breeze.

Note: Published in *Destiny Poets International* on 7 August 2024 and judged as one of the Highly Commended poems for August 2024.

Float Free – A Dandelion

No sense of
Self-aggrandisement
Self-entitlement
Arrogance
Hubris
Anger –
Float free.

Edges fraying
Melting in gold dust on sunbeams
A lightness I feel
As I float free
Melting in the gold dust on sunbeams
In the abundance of the universe.

The webs springing around my edges
Are not chains that contain me
But home to others who thrive with me
For we all live together.
This world is yours and this world is mine
For whatever time we are in it.

Float free
Free in the golden sunshine
Free on the breeze
Free in my being
Free in the universe of love.

Note: Published by *Setu Bilingual Journal*, November 2023

Float Free – A Snowflake

In the white of the winter, I gently wafted,
Wafted in the expanse of the cosmos,
Cosmos is the field of my journey,
Journey that knows no beginning or ending but just floating…
Floating free in the blue, a water drop am I.

I am the water drop that freezes,
Freezes around a mote of dust,
Dust journeying in the atmosphere,
Atmosphere that when very cold, my form transforms,
Transforms me into a silvery hexagonal snowflake.

Snowflake am I…
I owe my existence to the dust,
Dust around which my watery form settled,
Settled into beautiful crystalline fingers,
Fingers that fell into pre-ordained shapes.

Shapes that grew as more drops of water froze,
Froze around the nucleus of the dust,
Dust that pervaded the sky,
Sky to earth I drifted…
Drifted I with the winds.

Winter winds carried me through the cold,
Cold of the atmosphere that determined my form,
Form that I am blessed with—a gift.
Gift from the universe for bearing the coldness,
Coldness of the atmosphere determined my form.

Form that is at one with the universe,
Universe that takes my journey to the womb of the earth,

Earth that absorbs me gently when I fall,
Fall I with grace when I drift,
Drift I in peace with the universe.

Note: Published in the anthology *Winterful Whispers – Thaw the Frost*, Edited by Geethanjali Dilip, Avantika Vijay Singh, and Puja Mehta for the Yercaud Poetry Festival 2023.

Float Free – A Raindrop

Floating free in the universe
A raindrop am I
Free…free…free
Drifting with the winds,
Knowing no beginning
No end.
Landing on a leaf here
A flower there
An eave or an awning
I care not for the landing…
There I stay curled
For time infinitesimal
Reflecting the beauty of creation.
And, then I roll off
Pulled by the forces of nature
To submerge into creation,
From whence I came.

Fly Free – An Egret

In the golden dawn, the snowy egret flies free,
Greeting the rising sun early,
Its soaring flight, a divine sight,
Metamorphing with the light.

As it flies higher in the breeze,
My soul on its winged back it magically carries.
As it wings its powerful flight,
I fly to a greater height.

I look down and see the tops of the trees,
The flowers blooming among the leaves,
Carpets of yellow, mauve and white,
Below the trees I sight.

I look up and see,
Clouds stacked in a series,
Blushing roses amongst puffs of cotton white,
Scattered amidst sapphire skies in the golden light.

With the bird, I fly free,
Looking on creation with glee,
Free of attachments and desires trite,
That bind us to temporal delights.

A reminder that none can I carry,
In my sublime journey,
It is in the now to find delight,
For the soul to continue its winged flight.

In oneness with the bird, I float free,
In oneness with the clouds, I float free,
In an infinitesimal part of the universe, I delight,
Gold dust on sunbeams infinite.

Note: Published in *Destiny Poets International* on 28 July 2024

Float Free – Jasmine and Egret

Scattered like Jasmine flowers
That carpeted the green grass in white showers
Wade softly the snowy egrets in a line
Besides the blooming white Jasmine.

I see the birds by the Jasmine showers
Thinking they are the sky's flowers
And the flowers the earthly passerine
Each invested with the other's spirit in nature's shrine.

The flowers like birds flying for hours
Sitting on plants to rejuvenate their powers,
Blooming like souls on enlightenment's journey fine
Delighting in the day divine.

The birds fly free like flowers transcending bowers
With them fly I, free of any desires
My soul dancing in the dawn divine
Like gold dust on sunbeams shine!

Seeing the birds fly free in the morning hour
My anger, anguish, and anxiety empty by some magical power
With the birds my spirit aligns
Floating free in oneness like gold dust on sunbeams divine!

I become one with the flower,
One with the bird at this hour...
Feeling connected through power divine
An infinitesimal, interconnected part of nature's design.

quilling for
humanity

Within and Without

Sitting cross-legged in the park,
I drink in the sight of the
white Champa flowers against the grey skies,
besides the gracefully drooping red Bottlebrush,
where the spirited Gulmohar grows tall…
and the lush greenery is home to dancing peacocks.

The joyous colours transmit
vibrations of peace, joy, bliss.
Breathing in, I breathe in
peace, joy, bliss…
Breathing out, I breathe out
anger, frustration, sorrow…

As I close my eyes
My ears open…
My senses alive to the chirp of the birds
Cheep cheep, hoo-po hoo-po, piao piao
The birds' calls transmit
vibrations of *shanti*, peace, bliss…

I am a blissful being
at peace with nature,
at peace with myself…
A continuation of nature—
my being vibrates in rhythm
to nature's rhythm.

Note: Received the Certificate of Excellence 2024 for the Ratna Tripathi Memorial Award from the Asian Literary Society (ALS) for this poem.

What the World Needs...

The World needs to...
Build bridges of hope
To see dazzling designs in the kaleidoscope
Through the shards of glass
When life is at an impasse.

The World needs to...
Not be cocooned in the silken threads of desire,
For power, materialistic pleasures, and physical fires
But float free of the illusion
That leads to *insaaniyat's* corruption.

The World needs to...
Launch ships of humanity,
To sail into vistas of compassion and empathy,
Away from the sea of brutality
That drowns human respect and dignity.

The World needs to...
Light the torch of tolerance
So that of human spirit there is a renaissance
And the path burns bright with generosity,
Through the darkness of ignorance, prejudice, and bigotry.

The World needs to...
Not be weighed down by past actions
And anchored to the past by fulsome passions
But to flow in the waters of the present moment with clear reason
To create a diverse world for all seasons.

The World needs to...
Fly with faith into stratospheric heights,
To rejoice with the auroras' dancing lights
And iridescent hues

Of the rainbow clouds
When the horizon fills with storm clouds.

The World needs us...
To rise above ourselves
From the silos where each one dwells.
To dance in life's exuberance
And heal the world of malevolence.

Note: Published in *Yugen Quest Review*, Spring 2024, an issue dedicated to What Does the World Need? Guest Editor Dr Santosh Bakaya.

Awaken the Goddess Within

Rise! Find purpose and presence within.
Make life an extended inspiration
of the *Navaratri* celebration.
Awaken the Goddess within
and embrace the divine feminine!
Irrespective of gender, align
with the divine feminine!

Shailputri…
Daughter of the resilient mountain
blessed by birth with courage uncommon.
Symbolic of power and patience
to pursue goals with devotion.
She serves as a divine inspiration
to achieve goals and trust intuition.

Brahmacharini…
Who pursued in bare simplicity,
penance, sacrifice, and austerity
encourages inner strength and ability
to let go of much in humility
while walking the path of austerity
to achieve goals with equanimity.

Chandraghanta…
The Goddess of duality,
symbolic of charm, grace, and beauty,
when required dons a fearful identity.
The epitome of feminity
fights with terrifying ferocity…
This contrast is everyone's reality.

Kushmanda…
The divine light ray in the darkness,
the Creator of the Universe

with the light of her smile luminous,
and all gods and beings in the cosmos,
inspires similarly to dispel the darkness
with the light of love luminous.

Shailputri...
Daughter of the resilient mountain,
blessed by birth with courage uncommon,
symbolic of power and patience
to pursue goals with devotion.
She serves as a divine inspiration
to achieve goals and trust intuition.

Katyayani... Mahisasurmardini
The fiercest of Her incarnations,
Slayer of evil, Salutations!
She invokes courage and inspiration
to slay the evil of ego and toxic relations.
Made by the Gods' collaboration,
for teamwork, she inspires cooperation.

Kaalratri...
Slayer of Chanda-Munda demons,
inspires us to slay our demons,
slay ignorance and break stereotypes.
To drink up our desires in legions
like Her who drank the blood of Raktbeej demon,
to prevent it from multiplying into more demons.

Mahagauri...
The most divinely beauteous form,
in holy waters, she did transform,
from a dark form to a radiant form—
pure and compassionate, her reform.
Reminder for humanity to reform,
fairness and compassion, to be the norm.

Siddhidatri...
The bestower of *siddhi*
With Her wisdom and spirituality.
She, within each human the *nari*
in Ardhnareeshvar's divinity,
bringing 'wholeness', balance, and harmony
along with the divine masculine in sublimity.

Awaken the Goddess within
irrespective of gender; Awaken
devotion, austerity, resplendence, creation.
Destroy the darkness of negativity
borne from the ego, like the Mahisasurmardini.
Awaken the divine feminine
and bring peace and harmony to the world!

Note: Published in the *Setu Bilingual Journal* in October 2024 as a Special Attraction feature

The Gift of Tosali

Time flows on the sands
of Tosali where invisible hands
move the clock back to the distant past...
Greedy conquerors came furious and fast,
bringing death and destruction in their wake,
making existence opaque.

In evolution's undulating pace,
patterns often in reverse trace...
The conqueror became the conquered,
peace and serenity prospered,
"conquest by *dharma*"
became the new *karma*.

Long after empires bit the dust
and emperors lay in the sepulchre's silence hushed,
Tosali's gift to the world flourished,
compassion and humanity unfurled...
Blessed... the silence of serenity,
existence touched by purity.

Compassion, very much a requisite
in the new order of equity deficit.

Note: Published in *Toshali Anthology of Poetry* - 2025 for the Toshali Literature Festival, Bhubaneshwar.

Patterns

As frosty winds blow,
icy patterns of frost on windshields grow,
from trees to intricate leaves—
beauteous patterns, the ice weaves.

My warm breath I see escape
in the cold air in a shape,
like a small, puffed-up cloud—
patterns I see where none did abound.

As frosty winds blow,
the homeless shiver slow.
On the roads, they lie,
besides small fires under the open sky.

Sometimes on a *gurudwara's* steps...
At other times, under the flyovers complex.
They find shelter from the cold,
bundled under quilts tattered and old.

But the world works in its own fashion,
as unknown hands reach out in compassion,
distributing blankets to the destitute,
covering them with love resolute.
As frosty winds blow,
the patterns of compassion show...
Embracing the cold on footpaths and pavements,
in steaming cups of tea and other arrangements.

As frosty winds blow,
the dogs lie snuggled low,
on small hillocks of dug-out earth
for that warmth is their hearth.

As compassionate souls pass by,
jackets and food they supply.
In this world, as we pass by
in patterns of compassion, let us tie.

Note: This poem was published in *The Wise Owl* | *The Daily Verse* on 31 January 2025

Melt Away the Boundaries

See not the blemished skin,
see not the greying hair,
see not the jangling bellies,
judge not the external appearance
for they are merely illusions...

Where are the boundaries
that divide man from man,
but in the shallow pans
of our minds?
What a colossal waste
are these judgements
that birth duality,
when in reality
the universe knows only unity!

Melt away the barriers,
for nature knows no walls.
Melt into nature
to dance in exuberance
with the universe's diversity—
a musical extravaganza.

Who can judge
if a toucan's colours
are any prettier than a flamingo's?
Or the smell of petrichor finer than aspens'?
Melt away the barriers of the mind,
for they are just illusions…
and find yourself
lighter…
released from the burden of judgement.
Find yourself floating, like
gold dust on sunbeams…
warm sunshine on a winter morning.

A Time to Pause and Reflect

The heat and dust of summer
sink gradually below the horizon.
Raindrops glimmer
on leaves from chariots driven by Poseidon.

The misty monsoon morning,
made brighter
by the white Frangipani blooming,
flowing in abundance like a white river.

The spider's webs glimmer
like necklaces with tiny pearls...
against the greens, they appear clearer
with the raindrops that cling and curl.

Everything appears clearer
like a cleaned mirror.
Walking along Jasmine-lined pathways with spirits lighter,
on the beauty of nature, I ponder.

A time to pause and reflect...
What do we need for our happiness?
A patch of green, a stroll in nature with flowers bedecked,
that stirs our souls to dance... poetry perhaps.

How beautiful then is life in simplicity,
without the glitter of the glitterati.
What or who you wear such a triviality,
the heart can't be weighed with such superficiality.

Journey deep into the universe's immensity...
Into the inky, swirling, darkness of infinity,
and find, you are gold dust floating on sunbeams in serenity...
The fount of humanity,

with capacity to do deeds of monumental courage and nobility.
Let your thoughts be a clarion call for humanity,
be the radiance in the Universe's infinity.

Note: Published by *The Wise Owl* | *The Daily Verse*, 9 August 2024

On a Winter's Night

On a winter's night,
The darkness descends expeditiously,
The fog rolls in stealthily,
The chilled winds blow swiftly,
The mercury plummets rapidly...

The lady sits in front of the fireplace cozily,
Her needles twinning to the crackling logs noisily,
The gentlemen contemplate upon the wars moodily,
Downing their whiskey with the store-ordered snacks heartily,
Denouncing the state of the world loudly.

But the world outside shivers speedily,
The guards sit outside the high rise earnestly,
Their hands spread in front of feeble fires fully,
For while the world in the high rise sleeps soundly
They stay awake to the nightly clamour freely.

The delivery boys come to the high rise continually,
Facing the bitter cold on their bikes bravely,
Their faces wrapped in mufflers totally,
Sparing a glance towards the fires hungrily
But not wasting a minute before their delivery.

A lone e-rickshaw forays dauntlessly,
Looking for customers haplessly
Not a penny has he earned this day unfortunately
For who will venture out into the glacial winds willingly?
Who will douse the fires of his stomach stoutly?

Note: This poem was published by *The Wise Owl* | *The Daily Verse*, 29th January 2024

Gold Dust

The cartwheels of the economy spin on,
with wealth creation the golden morn'.
Tales of aggrandisement and displays of wealth,
replace stories of spiritual well-being and health.
Can joy be gained from worldly possessions?
Every earthly happiness knows a senescence.

Worldly pleasures but breed—
lust, ego, desire, and greed.
The very emotions to protect from...
Ticking time bombs,
dividing man from man
in humanity's giant clan.

Awaken your inner Athena,
to work in humanity's arena...
Fight against poverty, inequity, and inhumanity.
You... the gold dust in the Universe's infinity,
shining on sunbeams on the less fortunate
in actions compassionate.

Here, a girl steeped in appalling poverty
is empowered by education in all earnesty.
She breaks free from destiny's gross inequality...
And helps her family live a life of opportunity—
denied by birth the possibility,
but given now to transact a life with dignity.

There, a man trapped in the vicious cycle of loans,
weighed down by misery akin to heavy stones.
A little capital injected... the wind beneath his wings,
enabling him to wing free of debt's agonising strings,
empowering him to transform his life,
and, his duties to perform without strife.

Be the light and bring light,
to make lives shine bright.
Like gold dust on sunbeams,
sprinkle compassion in life's streams.
This, the legacy of our life—
Reduce suffering and strife...

The Orange Glow

On a ferry in the delta,
we floated alone on the blue.
A minute speck in the river
with none other in sight…no lights
either glowed on the distant coast.
A hush, a solitude imbued
as an orange glow suffused
the horizon after sunset.

As the ferry climbed into
the sunset, darkness descended.
And, yet the night lit up brightly…
Millions of stars came out to play,
shining big and bright in the night
as though the sky was washed clean.
The waters were moonwashed
in the pearly light of the moon.

My enchantment with the night grew
as I gazed around in wonder…
Silver waters in solitude
lapping in the silvery night.
I felt like a diminutive
speck of dust under the vast skies
floating timelessly on a boat
with a roof of the moon and stars.

In the crowded bazaar of life,
we often forget our minutia…
How like a speck of dust we are
in the Universe's largeness.
Then why the ego and the fights?
Why the gory wars and bloodshed?
Let the dust of our existence
add to the energy of life.

Note: Published in the *Literary Vibes – Edition CXLVII* (29 December 2024)

Yes, I Have Seen God!

In my darkest hour
As I stood drenched in misery's shower,
Came a ray of light
That comforted us with might.
His very presence like a lotus flower!

Was he God's messenger?
I could only think yes after the first encounter!
A confidence inspired his sight!
Hope once again burnt bright,
He had such quiet power!

The mind stilled its chatter,
Stilled the gyrations along the mental ladder!
Raheem... merciful and compassionate his light
Rehmani... God like his sight!
His presence made hope tower!

Faith reinforced by each hour
As miraculous deeds came to flower!
In gratitude, we remain for the fight
That put up our surgeon knight.
Yes, I have seen God!

His very presence like a lotus flower!
He had such quiet power!
His presence made hope tower!
Yes, I have seen God!
He is the Doctor
Raheem...Rehmani!

Note: Published in the *Literary Vibes, Edition CXLII* (28-June-2024)

A Visit to an Old Age Home

A visit to an old age home
will leave you in gloom,
wondering what is wrong with society.
Why do we leave our elderly
in the hands of strangers?

They are old and unsteady on their feet—
With pain in their knees,
barely can they stand.
With a walker, they trot a bit,
mostly willing to slumber the day away.

Some can't remember what day it is
and have flashes of memories from the past on good days.
They see you with eyes unseeing...
the hollowness of their gaze pricking your empty soul.
They call you with the names of their loved ones.

Oh! Where are they?
Where are these so-called loved ones
who leave their elders in an institution?
Consign them to the care of strangers
because they have not the time or space for them.

You say you have not the room in your house
but all that is needed is space in your heart.
Give not the luxury of your money for their care
but give the luxury of your time rare.
A little love, a little respect, a little regard...

It is the circle of life to be cared for and to care.
If today we are on our feet standing fair,
it is because someone cared for us during our childhood.
Has not the time come to repay the debt for good?
For what are they if not aged babies?

We need not brazenly follow ideas from other countries
as though everything they did was superior.
The culture of our own country is good...
We learned that divinity rests in every form.
Come, it is time to pay back gratitude for what they did.

Raise your hands in *sewa*
for rare is such an opportunity.
What use is the ringing of bells and blowing of conch shells
when the real Gods and Goddesses of our lives
lay languishing?

Note: Published in *Free Voice* on 30 October 2023

The Selfie

Self-love they say
and the selfies go on display!
The phones most prized
for cameras glorified.
In much demand are apps rare
that make you slim and fair.

Filters that change you,
make you softer... fairer,
in keeping with society's definition of beauty.
Dare we not like ourselves for what we are?
Dare we not accept our outer blemishes?
When we have stopped looking at our inner ones.

Encashing on human frailty,
pandering to hubris and vanity,
is the trend of the selfie!
Capturing moments as we are
or as we wish to be?
Perpetuating an endless cycle of desires!
And, desires are the root cause of suffering!

Why this obsession with the outer self?
Is that not a rather empty construct of one self?
Does not self-love include the person within—
the person inside the skin?
Make the selfie for self-love not an excuse...
Inculcate self-love with a low threshold
for toxic relationships and abuse!

Let not fashion's passion for vanity
construct walls between humanity.
Rise above the narrow constricts of discrimination
above self-punishment and recrimination.

See the wonder within and in one another
for only then can we create a wonderful world.

Note: Published by *Free Voice* on 11 November 2023

Ubuntu

It was the year 2020
when the dreaded virus made an entry.
The most fearsome time in history,
how we fell to the pandemic, a real mystery.
Schools shut, trains shut, shops shut,
files gathering dust.
Isolation, the only solution—
building walls between people, the new resolution.

And yet,
came forward…
The best of humanity,
irrespective of their immunity.
They showed compassion,
distributing free ration,
to those who lacked daily subsistence.
Giving every assistance
to those who contracted the virus…
Caring not for themselves in this crisis.

They showed interconnectedness of spirit,
serving others without limit.
Running free oxygen banks
for people of all ranks.
In hospitals, they treated people,
even while falling to the virus lethal.
Yes, there were shortages
due to black marketing, there were outages.
But they worked ceaselessly,
helping strangers to stem the tide of death miraculously.

Masking up, they broke the distance...
And assisted human existence.
While teaching went online,

there were those who lived below the line,
and lacked the means to go online.
There were those who taught offline,
ensuring that literacy did not die…
Even if it took a backseat when
survival itself was in short supply.

As I remember the harrowed times,
I realise...
I am because of you,
And you are because of us.
Someone cared, someone respected,
Someone showed compassion,
Someone took the first step…
Someone followed, making it the norm.
Someone broke the normal
And made a new normal.
We all are because of each other...
And to me, that's Ubuntu.

Note: This poem was written to the prompt "Use a beautiful, unusual word from another language and write a poem so that its meaning comes through" given by Baisali Chatterjee Dutt on 1 April 2024. I chose the word Ubuntu, from traditional African philosophy that translates to "I am because you are, you are because we are."

being woman

Set Me Free

Tie me not in chains of gold
for my worth is manifold.
My golden anklets moor me
to a cage with no key.

Set me free,
and let me be...
An uncaged bird
with dreams unfettered.

Give me an education
that improves my life's station.
On anyone else, make me not dependent,
my life's path, let me carve independent.

Give me an education
that births an ambition
and the ability to soar the heavens...
not be held ransom by social customs.

A few more years in the chrysalis,
some time for transformation in bliss,
better equipped to handle relationships,
and negotiate the perilous channels of life like skilled ships.

I am not anyone's chattel
to be levied with taxes in battle.
I am a human, too, with potential,
not merely a womb to populate exponential.

Tie me not
into youthful matrimony's knots.
Give me a chance...
in the golden skies to dance.

Set me free,
and let me be...
an uncaged bird
with dreams unfettered.

Note: Published by the *Free Voice* in August 2024

The Living Durga

Autumn heralds *agomani*...
waking to the sound of the *dhaak*,
dancing the *dhunuchi*,
with burning clay pots in hand.
It is the annual homecoming
of the Goddess Durga—
an intensely awaited time
signalled by the
shiuli blooming,
kaash phool ripening
to a pearly whiteness...
the harbinger of autumn.

The Goddess comes to earth,
staying among men and women.
For ten days
the fervour of worship
wafts in the air
with the fragrance of incense.
She is worshipped
and then given a teary farewell.

But what of the Goddess
who stays on Earth?
What of the ordinary woman—
the woman on the street?
Is she not to be worshipped?
Is she not to be nurtured
like the daughter who came home?
Is she only to be used shamelessly
and cast aside carelessly?
What conscience permits
the heinous crime of a woman's dishonour?

Beware! Beware!
She is not a *bechari*.
She is an incarnation of the Goddess
and will return
to seek justice,
if not directly
then indirectly.
We all pay for our sins—
our *karma*,
in this very lifetime…
Justice will find its way!

Beware!
Beware the Goddess!
Beware of *karma*!
Justice will find its way.
Do good and release goodness.
Worship the Goddess,
not for ten days,
but each day…
Worship the Goddess on earth.

Note: Published by *Yugen Quest Review*, Preservation Part 2, September 18, '24: Justice, Safety, Equality

Who Am I?

Who am I?
Am I the woman in the mirror,
Draped in her nine yards of finery,
Eyes filled with dreams for a lifetime?
Am I the woman with a belly swollen,
Nourishing a life in my womb,
Or cradling a baby in my arms?
Am I the sarong-clad woman on the beach,
Or the one in pants at a corporate meet?

Does it matter what I wear?
Why does my spirit have to be bound by what I wear?
Why do my physical dimensions have to define my existence?
What does it matter whether I hold a pen or a baby?
Look beyond what I look, what I wear.
It is a very shallow existence,
Indeed, an empty existence to live just for the mirror.
Time changes everything...

Within the blink of a cosmic eye, I will change...
Rich one day, poor another,
Thin one day, fat another,
Young one day, old another.
Walking miles one day, sitting on a chair, another day.
Will the change in time change who I am?
Will a sensuousness make me more tolerable if I am cranky?
Will I be esteemed less if my cup does not level up to society's brim?

Does a youthful face matter
If your spirit is bound in chains?
Open your eyes and see me for who I am—
Look beyond my fading eyes and crinkling skin.

Look within...
Into my soul,
See me for what I am
Before I escape this form.

Note: Published by *Yugen Quest Review*, Preservation Part 2, September 18, '24: Justice, Safety, Equality

Is Pinkness a Thing?

The sky blushes pink
in incredible ink
in anticipation of an exquisite dawn.

The buds lay curled in pink
as the dew falls distinct
in anticipation of a gorgeous blossom.

Jaipur—the Pink City,
Washed by a Maharana in the colours of hospitality,
in anticipation of a royal visit.

Nurseries, too, are painted pink
in a blink,
in anticipation of a girl child.

However, the explosion of pink...
the Barbies and the fake mink
made Pink sit up and think.

When did I get associated with gender?
Was it when I was blushing tender?
When did I become a social construct?
A woman is nature's greatest strength,
not one colour, but an amalgamation of all in her depth.

Is the extended celebration of pink,
an exploitation to hear the monies clink?
A stereotyping that needs to be broken?

Note: This poem was written to the prompt, "Is Pinkness a thing?" given by Amita Paul.

"A Girl and Not a Boy"

"A girl and not a boy"
read she in the gaze of those who went by
working on the farm as a daily wage labourer
in the heat and dust, helping her father,

she felt heavily burdened
with the weight of disappointment
in the gaze of those who cast
pitiable glances at her till the last,

it furrowed within her
a fury so sure
that she determined to show them all
through the female gaze, a nuanced portrayal...

a graduate in a village,
to the big city, she hiked to come of age
learning digital literacy
without which there were no jobs literally,

and then dawned the day,
when time to her did sway
and she got a fat-paying job
with which many things she bought

back to the village she went
presenting gifts to her parents,
meeting respectful glances from the crowd—
"A girl and not a boy" made the village proud

Note: This is based on a real-life story from a village in Andhra Pradesh, attesting to a change in attitudes.

A River of Vermillion

In the precious parting
of her hair's midst, flowing...
a river of vermillion
that gave flight to dreams million,
bangles tinkling on wrists
anklets dancing in silvery mists,
her face wreathed in smiles of delight
reflected in the vivid hues of her sari bright,

but,
flames from her husband's funeral pyre,
lit grief within her like a raging fire,
engulfing her in a loss so deep
that life slipped into a miserable sleep...
while the fire consumed her husband's life,
it consumed, too, her life,
her very identity,
and she became a shell entity,
standing in twilight's somnolence
surrendering to the darkness' dominance...

however, a still darker fate awaited her—
since no longer flowed midst her hair, the vermilion river,
broken harshly were the tinkling, delicate bangles
stilled the echoes of her anklets,
snatched from her were colours,
and life dissolved like the mist's vapours...
she stood with head tonsured, spirit bereft,
grieving for the loss of her identity in time's test,

and now started a new journey—
abandoned... disowned... outcast...
deprived of love and support
when she needed it most...
clawing in the dust—

for a morsel of food,
a morsel of affection,
a morsel of her identity...

fie on those
that snatch a woman's identity,
not the vermillion in her hair's parting
but she herself, is a river...
let her flow free in the river of time
carving her own identity

She – 1

History showed many a woman
sustain domination and abuse
from the patriarchal society and her man—
"For the children" was always her excuse.

She writhed in misery,
all for the fear of society,
and lived on life's periphery
with her closest ally—anxiety.

But then she resolved to let go of her fear
and burn her bridges.
Her fear burnt in a glorious conflagration on the pier...
Cleansed by fire, emerged a new 'her' prodigious.

She was *Shakti*, the female energy...
She was fearless, timeless, and danced
with the universe in glorious synergy.

Note: This poem was written to the prompt, "Write a sonnet to this quote by Dylan Thomas – When one burns one's bridges, what a very nice fire it makes" given by Dr Santosh Bakaya on 8 April 2024

She – 2

I was most taken
by a painting of Leonid Afremov unmistaken...
The painting of a flamenco dancer,
who conveyed the romance of life within her.

Swirls of oil on canvas
made up the ruffles of her dress,
symbolising the colours of a woman's life
by the strokes of the knife.

She held herself straight
with the grace of strength that a woman has innate.
And, yet she danced with fluid motion
as flowed through her, jeweled emotions.

What quiet power she spread
in the turn of her head.
What passion she held
as the music swelled
and the dance within her filled!

What power it is to be a woman strong!
Strong enough to stand up to wrong!
Gentle enough to flow sublime
in the river of Life divine!

Note: This poem was written in response to the prompt, "Write a poem about a piece of art or sculpture that deeply moved you," which I gave on 24 April 2024. The poem was featured in the Spring 2024 edition of *Yugen Quest Review*.

The Period

I used to be tall in my life's initial period.
Then I was visited by the period
And that was the end of my growth period.

From being the tallest girl
I became the shortest without fail.
From being a backbencher
I became a frontbencher
In class eight.
And I hated that fate.

You see, there is a different psychology
To a front and backbencher's physiology.
While at the back I could giggle and roar
In the front, I could do that no more.

Instead, I was expected to be studious
And always be seated on my gluteus
Answering the teacher's questions in each period.
Oh! How I blamed my period
For the end of a carefree period!

Note: This poem was written to the prompt, "My bench in Class 8" given by Lily Swarn on 6 April 2024.

A Relic

As time flows by,
flow by many memories
some to seek subterranean routes
in my sub-conscious, unseen
even as new experiences take root
blooming in my consciousness.

Flowing in the subterranean cave system
of my memories,
were my grandparents
with whom I spent much of my childhood.
Till I chanced upon a relic…
a painting of my grandmother, my *nani*.

And then, the lost river
sprung to life…
with a tidal force.
A parallel universe
danced in the air
from over a century before.

She, a beauteous rose
with roses on her cheeks
in a deep rose saree…
The saree she held close to her heart
for it was the bridal finery
in which she started her marital life at 14.

The portrait made, from a photograph
my *nana* always carried.
On the streets of Italy, wedded the photo
to the roses of my *nana's* memory.

And she emerged... draped in the wedding saree,
the *palla* so graciously covering her head.

A century later...
I wonder what her dreams were...
What her life was like
raising children alone
as she waited for a husband,
far away on the Western Front.

Framed in time
in a golden frame...
A golden heart...
Resplendent in the infinite
well-spring of her heart
where lived love!

The embroidery on the border
a reminder in the tapestry of my memories...
How her nimble hands taught mine
to transform a blank landscape,
with riotous embroidery into a dreamscape!
With your own hands, your happiness to shape!

Assailed by the fragrance of this timeless past,
I am served a rich repast
of emotions and nostalgia.
I hear the strains of laughter,
silent voices in my head
as around her lavish spread, they congregate.

I see her face
not the one in the portrait,
but the one I knew well...
The wrinkled one
that offered
kindness, love, and comfort...

And, I know a gentle ache,
a chasm that can never be filled with time.
But like the subterranean river,
that disappears somewhere
and emerges somewhere else...
So do my memories,
this time, triggered by a relic.

Note: This poem, written for my grandmother, is part of *The Relic*, an anthology edited by Dr Meenakshi Mohan and Dr Santosh Bakaya.

The Sunshine

You are the sun transcendental,
Around whom revolve, we planets, coincidental
Life's path we trace in our orbits,
But it is you who holds us close strongest.

You who illumines our lives quite
With your intellect and love bright.
You who radiates effulgence
Taking on life's trials with magnificence.

The legacy of army blood
Courses through your veins in torrential flood.
You adventured through life with might,
Making a home out of boxes infinite.

You, our Sun, bestow warmth and love—
Your hand-knitted sweaters, a treasure trove.
Your intelligence and skill cabled into the design
Infusing every piece with your heart's rhythm divine.

You, the centre of our universe
Who loved and nurtured the blank verse,
Knitting all family members, diverse
Into a joyful metaverse.

At ease in high echelons,
Or cooking feasts in the kitchen,
Or helping a neighbour quietly,
You built a strong community.

You, the presiding deity
Of the *navagrahas*' piety,
You, the essence of our identity...
From you, springs logophilia in its entirety.

Surya Namaskara honours the Sun
With 12 yoga postures in salutation.
For all the forms you spun:
Charm, grace, intellect, strength, love, gentleness, and fun
Resilience, care, creativity, courage, and compassion,
O Mother, accept my humble salutation!

The Harvest Moon

O, Harvest Moon lustrous,
Immense and luminous,
With her halo of gold,
Shining light manifold.

Harvest moon,
Heralding autumn,
Celebrating summer,
Embracing a new season.

You are the Harvest moon…
In your life's autumn,
Celebrating summer,
Embracing a new season.

Strangers were we,
Tossing upon life's sea,
Till destiny played its part,
Making me your daughter by heart.

Always considerate
And compassionate…
No demands traditional,
Giving love, unconditional.

From you, I learned a time
Simple and yet sublime…
Simplifying the complexity,
Contentment in austerity.

You walk with your head high
Under the big, blue sky,
With the courage to dare
A life of convictions rare.

And to the Harvest moon,
We owe deep gratitude,
Letting us harvest life's crops
By her bright light,
Late into the night.

Note: This poem is written for my mother-in-law. It was published in Literary Vibes – Edition CL (28 Feb 2025).

Dear Daughter

I am thankful dear Daughter...
You chose me as your mother
in this lifetime,
to fulfill a soul-connect sublime.

The verses that threshed in me,
found mellifluous song in you.
My thinking, often muddled,
found clear flow within you.

Shedding the baggage of privilege
like a monsoon-fed river, I emerge,
while you flow steady
like the Himalayan rivers mighty.

The colours I struggled to see
burst into rainbows within you.
The philosophies I grappled with
found a merger of ethics and aesthetics within you.

You grew from within me
but you grew much beyond me.
Such is the dichotomy of life...
those who think we make, make us.

You complete me in ways I didn't see,
didn't expect to be...
And yet, leave me free,
to live my life, touched by you.

And, I am thankful to you
for all the conversations and thoughts,
the emotions and love...
The 'experience of mothering'
mothered in me.

Where Dreams Take Flight

Upon the shifting sands of time, it stands,
a vision of strength, a sight grand.
In winter's golden light, it gleams
giving sturdy beams to your dreams.

A vision fit for Olympus
made surely by a Hephaestus
none other than yourself,
the brick-and-mortar version of yourself.

Your thoughts sparkle silver
like the Orlias river,
flowing swiftly and clearly—
seeing facts distinctly.

Your wisdom and courage
pay Athena homage.
Your gift to see reason,
powers you for all seasons.

I see in your house grand,
vast spaces for dreams to expand,
reflecting your image
etched upon time's page.

In this house open to the sky,
Apollo drives his chariot by…
Alighting through the window space,
illuminating minds in golden grace.

And in the silver night,
Artemis weaves dreams bright,
balancing Apollo's fiery illumination
with intuitive grace to make you a celebration.

In this house of your dreams,
bathed in golden sunbeams and silver moonbeams,
may love and bliss forever abide
and, from strength to strength, you glide.

Note: This poem is written for my friend, Dr Vandana Marwah.

A Water Nymph

A modern-day water nymph are you…
Fitted in your tracks
Sitting on the rocks,
Surveying your surreal expanse
That flows blithely beside you in a dance.

So fluid and graceful are you…
Here you sit on the banks
And there you morph with the ranks
Worshipping the gentle waters
Divining their tranquillity for your inner altars.

Gracefully swimming with the flow,
The ancient songs flowing in your veins,
Burbling with the mystical knowledge,
Of nature's beauty and eternity
At one with the divine forces.

Naiad,
With such grace you preside over the corporate waters,
Often swimming gracefully upstream,
Against the current...
Such quiet strength in your long limbs.
Such rigor and discipline in your gentle disposition.

Tender-hearted and compassionate you are,
Melting like the silver moon
In the ripples of the river at night tide,
To encompass all in the benevolence of your beatitude
Stemming from the infinite wells of your empathy.

With such fluidity you cross the borders
Between personal and professional waters
Bringing to the table, a professional exemplary
Bringing to the home, an unmatched identity
Naiad... you are the modern-day woman!

Note: Published by *Lothlorien* on 1 January 2024

The Nightingale

behold the nightingale of Yercaud
a land carved surely by God,
melodies at dawn, she trills
over vales and hills—
Geethatmaa, the songs of her soul
that wash over her whole
in *Atmatarang*, ripples of emotion
stirring universal love's ocean…

not unlike Wordsworth's Solitary Reaper is she
"breaking the silence of the seas"—
the silence of silos,
for she believes
poetry connects the world
and often sits curled
in *Swapna Geetham*, golden dreams,
curating festivals and anthologies that gleam…

in the silver mists of time,
she chants verses sublime
in surrender to the divine
that like gold dust on sunbeams shine
in emerald forests
Aaranyageetham, where she rests
singing with timeless grace
jewelled songs, *Mani Geetham*

The Mahasagar

She's not a river
who trembles
seeing the ocean.
But she is the ocean herself...
the stately, calm ocean...
An ocean of love
in which play
the tides
glinting in the sunshine
with the gentle breeze.
An ocean of love
in whose lap frolick
many beings...
all feeling the warmth
of her love.

The tides...
they come and go.
The rivers...
they empty
into her,
but she remains...
The ocean,
the mahasagar
of love...
All encompassing
All knowing
Unperturbed
Gently flowing...

An Ode to Santosh Bakaya

a wizard is she
with words bubbling free
from her invisible hat,
under which sat
a whole universe
in multiverse...
goblins, squirrels, lizards,
came tumbling out in a veritable blizzard

she howled with laughter under her bed
as prompts came dancing from her head...
her eyes danced in glee,
stumping mere mortals like me
with prompts
more delicious than croissants

endowing inanimate objects
with sympathetic prospects
is her specialty,
and so steadfast her receptivity...
rocks, porcelain, lizards, sinks,
there is nothing from which her mind shrinks

so prolific a writer is she
that before you count to three
another poem or book holds you in thrall
and that's not all—
she writes with deep empathy
about the homeless, destitute, and needy

she'll faithfully read all authors
to mine from her rich coffers
jewelled blurbs and forewords

that are much treasured;
a wizard indeed is she
making many writers break free,
from their chains of seriousness,
sobriety and sombreness,
to dive deep into the fount of creativity
and drink from the chalice of spontaneity

Note: This poem was first written to the prompt, "Write a poem for Santosh Bakaya, the idyllic author, dreamer, conjurer, who carries rabbits, squirrels, prompts, and goblins in her hat..." given by Smeetha Bhoumik on 20 April 2024. The poem was published in *Yugen Quest Review* in Spring, 2024.

The Rare Flower

Flowering in the Anthropocene,
a late epoch in the geological timescale,
is Amita Paul.

Where man is blamed
for causing climate change,
is the Anthropocene.

Where man is blamed
for the destruction of the earth,
is Anthropocene.

But in this epoch flowered
a Poet and earth lover incomparable,
like the rare Neelakurinji that flowers once in 12 years.

Her pen brought to life
the beauty of the earth through the rare Neelakurinji,
and set me yearning to see it in its next flowering.

Note: This poem was written to the prompt, "Write Tercets for Earth and Amita Paul, the incomparable Earth lover (at least five)" given by Smeetha Bhoumik on 22 April 2024. The poem was published by *Yugen Quest Review* in Spring 2024.

Pearl of Courage

in the ocean's embrace
where waves rage and tempests race,
a tiny pearl thrust to life
from a grain of dust's strife

in the shallows did it dwell
coasting tides that rise and swell,
hearing the ocean's siren song
flying in the breeze long

and then one day, it was no longer free
in an oyster's shell, it came to be,
trapped in time,
no escape to climb

layer upon layer of nacre
time, the oyster, wrapped around her,
the pressure grew
buried deep within the blue

in her solitary confinement, she grew a stony heart
though unbeknown to her, nature crafted her with great art,
strength and patience woven into her texture
wisdom her vesture

and then cracked the shell one day,
in the deep, dark abyss, she felt the warmth of the golden ray...
and out emerged the gleaming wonder
a pearl, they called her

born from storms, shaped by stars,
still bearing the scars,
she grows strong and bright,
with each passing day and night

a lustrous wonder is she
warm, graceful, and free...
journeying across the river of dreams
like gold dust on sunbeams

Note: This poem was written as a birthday gift to my friend, Neha Bothra.

The Swan Couple

there once lived a swan couple
devoted to each other as they cosily huddled
flying together across sapphire skies
seeing the golden dawn of a new sunrise

life sailed across a river of dreams
carrying echoes of songs that gleam
smiles shimmering on the shores of love
as they cooed like a pair of doves

life flew on the whispers of the breeze
a gentle, fleeting rustle of the leaves
in the hush of twilight's solitude
they heard the symphony of the interlude

till time, cruel time
snatched him in life's prime
and she was left alone in the twilight
alone in the grief of her soul's long, dark night

she cried and cried
copious tears on time's tide
her heart breaking each time Facebook brought back her reveries
and mine breaking to see her memories

and then one day, she spotted Cygnus
the Swan constellation in the northern sky,
seeing her mate in the silver stardust,
she smiled, silver-haired, and tried to adjust...

making peace with grief in her heart
while honouring love that would never depart

Pandorathon

Whither Goes the Love Letter

To love I am a testament...
Birthed from its silken sentiment
Onto an elegant silk napkin,
In the fabric of life wrapped therein.

Beautiful black writing
With cursives delighting ...
As secrets come spilling
Woven into the tapestry of life thrilling.

A document of human emotion,
When the heart is in commotion
Dancing on its own volition
In love's big blue ocean.

A love letter am I
Written on a table napkin with a sigh...
Lovingly pressed to the lips
To derive comfort from the scripts.

To be viewed with pleasure
When life takes a measure
To be the bosom companion
When love blossoms wild like the banyan.

And, then as the ecstasy of love wanes
As the business of life waxes
To be cast away in the shadows of time...
Where cobwebs hang over rainbows sublime.

To be viewed occasionally,
And be drenched with tears sporadically
And, then along life's dusty lanes
To be relegated to the bylanes...
Such is my fate.

A relic am I
From an age gone by...
A memory of happy, heady times
Now an embarrassment
Stuck in time's limbo...
Too precious to be thrown away,
Too emotional to be visited when
Love's volatile volcano cools into placid seas.
Just like love...
Tucked in a corner of precious memories
As life surges ahead with the roar of the seas.

Note: This poem was written to the prompt "The fate of a love letter written on a paper napkin" on 1 April 2024.

A Crystal Ballerina

Carved in crystal
stood upon a pedestal
a beautiful ballerina—
Gazing beyond the patina
that esconced society
to not see beyond its own satiety.

"Could they not see,
how real was she?"
As she stood there
frozen in the market square,
she saw the little girl
who did a twirl,
gazing up adoringly at her
determined to be a ballerina in the future.

She saw the old man
abandoned by his clan
sitting by the small fire
gazing at her with ire
shivering in the cold,
while she stood quite controlled.
But quite miraculously,
the empathy in her eyes drove out his melancholy.

She saw the woman cleaning the room
to whom clung a cloak of gloom
except when she gazed at the ballerina joyously.
Stretching out her arms graciously,
pulling herself into an arabesque
that gave her grace statuesque
to fight with fate for a chance
from poverty to advance.

For her abilities to inspire and appeal,
the ballerina believed that she was real!
She knew many crystal ballerinas lived
broken, dead, deprived
living and yet frozen
while she frozen, evoked an emotion.
Then how could she not be real?

Note: This poem was written to the prompt, "A crystal ballerina who thinks she is real" given on 2 April 2024.

Rattle's Tattle

Rattle, rattle, rattle...
Went the skeletons
Tattle, tattle, tattle...
Sighed the closet,
Tired of all the prattle.
For centuries had the closet borne,
Skeletons that would have left the family torn.

Finally in defiance,
The closet broke its silence
"No more shall I bear the cross
Of your moral certitude's loss.
No more can you be absolved of your crime
And sit in hallowed sunshine."

You and yours showed me no gratitude.
But kept on increasing the magnitude,
Of crimes unspeakable
Of chaos palpable.
Kept piling high the skeletons
And made me the beast of your burden.

You poisoned the fount of goodness that one holds sacred,
With the seed of greed and hatred.
Releasing anarchy
Into the waters of humanity,
Such that progress stands today at a crossroads
Because corruption explodes.

My chest is heavy with your beastiality
But no longer can flourish this partiality!
I am weary of the screams
That resound within my beams.
And long to live free
Take onus of your actions is my earnest plea.

Spare me!!!
Live a wondrous life of abundance
Not of selfish indulgence
Live in gratitude and peace
And you will find your joys increase.
These are the greatest treasures
And not those of worldly pleasures!

Note: This poem was written to the prompt, "The soliloquy of a closet that is tired of skeletons residing within it" given on 3 April 2024.

A Story of Lights

Chandelier: I live in the palace
adding grandeur matchless
to the magnificence
with my incandescent luminescence.

Lamp: I am made from the earth
and light many a humble hearth.
Not for me opulence
but great providence.

Chandelier: Within me glow a million lights,
I dispel the darkness of the night.
Rainbows shimmer
from my crystal's glimmer.

Lamp: No rainbows spring from me,
no light magnifies from me.
I stand alone in my solitude
in the universe's magnitude.

Chandelier: That is rather a sad state.
With my friends, happiness I create
as in synchrony, we glow
on all those dancing below.

Lamp: Your light shines on those born in privilege
while my light falls on those, who know not such a grandiose image.
However, blessed are they,
for the empathy and compassion, they display.

Chandelier: I am an object of immense beauty,
appreciated for my grace by those who know me.
Who sings your praise?
How do you amaze?

Lamp: I am minuscule in the Universe's vastness,
my light a brief flare in the darkness.
Not for me the plaudits of ovation
but the piety of devotion.

My small size endows me with mobility
to be a vehicle of divinity.
I'm often set afloat in the river with flowers
to honour the Gods for their life-giving and sustaining powers.

Chandelier:
It's my privilege to learn of your ways.
It's not necessary to be big on displays!

Note: This poem was written to the prompt, "A conversation between a chandelier and a lamp" given on 4 April 2024.

A Smitten Kitten

Meow, meow...
Mews a kitten sleepy eyed
snuggling against her mother's side.
Curled up in her mother's warm embrace,
loving, warm licks lavish her face.

Encouraged by her mother's caresses,
she opens her eyes and stretches.
And sees her beloved mother's face,
her face with love trace.

She purrs delightfully with pleasure
and opens her eyes fully to the treasure.
Lavishing love upon her mother
her gaze beyond the mother wanders.

The sun's first rays melted the dawning
with youthful roses, the sky blushing.
Silver ribbons weaving along violet edges
as the sky with orange orb dresses.

The kitten rolls on her back
to give the orange orb a good whack.
But finds her paw passing through empty space
and her mother guffaws from her place.

Puzzled...the kitten watches...
The skies rippling with colour swatches,
the clouds racing,
her friendly paws evading.

Meow, meow
Purrs the kitten
With her first morn' utterly smitten.

Note: This poem was written to the prompt, "The reaction of a kitten on seeing her first sun ray" given on 4 April 2024.

Snowy Tales

A snowman stood lonely
Watching the scene distantly
Of the merriment of children
Throwing snowballs at each other and run.

A snowball came in his direction
From which there was no deflection.
And then with great impertinence
It started questioning the snowman's existence.

Snowball: Why do you stand so serious?
With just a smirk on your face mysterious?
Does not the children's laughter
Make you smile with all the banter?

Snowman: You twerp!
Not two minutes old and pumping questions galore.
Well! If you must know, of laughter there is no dearth.
I absorb the joviality and banter in my girth.

Suddenly the air vibrated
With the tension generated.
And a snowball came excitedly whooshing,
Hitting the snowman like an arrow
And knocking off his nose narrow.

Snowman: Arrrgghhh... Watch where you are going...
Mindlessly hurtling...
What pleasure can be there in such an action?
That hurts others in such a fashion...

Snowball: I am not an instrument for hurting
But one for loving.
My destiny is not my own.
I am born to be thrown.

Snowman: My destiny, too, is not my own
However, great kindness have I known.
From loving hands am I shaped
With people's clothes am I draped.

Snowball: No drapes for me
Only mirth and glee...
In the course of my short flight
I experience life's greatest delight
For I am alive
Into my being, I arrive.

Snowman: In that, we share great similarity
Shaped by another's hand for posterity
Born from the winter snow
For a short time, we glitter and glow
And when our time is done
Back into the water cycle are we spun,
To fall as snow one day.
To be shaped into existence one day!

Note: This poem was written to the prompt, "Conversation between a snowman and a snowball" given on 6 April 2024.

Granny's Wicker Trunk

Decades later I'm reminded of my granny's wicker trunk
lying in the attic.
I discovered it one day while playing *Chor Sipahi*
where the *sipahi* has to discover the *chor* (thief).
On that occasion, I was the *chor*,
hiding in the attic.

While waiting to be caught out, my eyes fell on the wicker trunk,
which seemed to have great character and spunk.
It beckoned me, begged me "to open".
On silent feet, I crept up to it and tugged the lock that lay broken.
In that, I found my *nani's* bridal saree
that was moth-bitten to a degree.
Yet, kept lovingly for her to be wrapped in on her last journey.

There were treasured pieces of bedcovers,
embroidered with many flowers.
Designs from generations past,
a legacy of embroidered linens amassed.
Digging past, I found some black-and-white photographs
of a lady with immense beauty
whom I had a hard time relating with my wrinkled granny.

Discovering that I had discovered her treasured trunk
my *nani* left some change for me in its depths that clunk.
She encouraged me silently to dip into this largesse.
And every time I had a headache or stomach ache or any other upsets,
small change found its way into my hands
to be exchanged for sweets in the market stands.
My mother could never understand how my aches
miraculously disappeared with visits to the attic.
But my granny just winked and kept up the facade to the last.

Note: This poem was written to the prompt, "Granny's wicker trunk lying in the attic" given on 7 April 2024.

Fairytales Are Not for Frogs

A frog sat outside a window chintz
when a mother was reading
the story of the frog Prince
to her daughter in the late evening.

That night it rained and rained,
the streets were flooded,
the gardens were flooded
but the frog remained in his dreams, mesmerised.

He swam in the waters.
Convinced he was the Frog Prince,
he anointed himself with the royal waters
for that's what he thought they were when he rinsed.

His chest swelling with great pride
the frog was filled with gumption.
Its crown was not to be denied
was now its assumption.

But more than the crown,
it awaited the kiss
from a maiden in town
who would bestow on him the supreme bliss.

He sat on a submerged root
expectantly looking up at maidens who passed that route,
raising his puffed-up cheeks upwards
defying them to kiss him as they bent downwards.

The birds were quite amused
by the frog's identity crisis.
They explained to the frog that he was quite confused
and no human would rescue him from his crisis.

But the frog continued to croak belligerently
until the little girl who heard the fairytale
came up and kicked his rump magnificently
and said, "Fairy tales are not for real."

"They are more about morality
and espousing good behaviour.
So don't expect any validation from others in reality.
Be your own saviour."

Note: This poem was written to the prompt, “A Frog suffering from an identity crisis” given on 9 April 2024.

Letting Off Steam

What has the 21st century brought to us?
Cars creating so much fuss!
Cars that run into lakhs and crores
And cause much woes!

There was once a time
That I ruled the roads prime.
We did just fine at that time!
At a fraction of the dime.

My only counterpart was the ambassador
That had a larger perimeter.
But where sleekness was called
I was the one recalled.

Families bundled into us
Happy families that had much to discuss.
On long trips, we went
Climbing hills and vales a hundred percent.
Mirth and laughter were our accompaniment,
To the present moment.

In my time, the world was united,
Into haves and have-nots not divided
Today a man's value derives
From the brand he drives.

Today, the roads are a mess
With branded cars vrooming to impress.
Sadly, these youngsters of today
Will only know speed and luxurious display
And not the camaraderie born of humbleness
With a life led with some purpose.

Note: This poem was written to the prompt, "A fiat car's monologue" given on 13 April 2024.

The Bard and the Bird

Squawk, squawk
Went a strange bird as it tried to talk
To Driftwood Ashore
Who the current swept ashore.

But Driftwood Ashore who had just swept in with the stream
Was in somewhat of a steam.
"Begone bird", he muttered.
But the bird only angrily sputtered.

Now the mood was brewing
For a battle royal in the offing
Each looked at the other warily
And took in the other's measure testily.

The bird squawked and flew
In circles over driftwood Ashore who willed it to stew
Stoically, he thrashed his arms
Not presenting the bird with his ample charms.

The bird was flabbergasted
Who was this who was not exhausted
After wrestling with the tide
Whose spirit none could subside.

Squawk, squawk
He squawked louder
And flew in closer
For a bold look anew
Of this strange driftwood that came walking in from the blue.

Squawk, squawk
He squawked harder
And tried to dive in closer

But Driftwood Ashore who was used to a little notoriety
Being written about by the Significant League's fraternity
Turned and squawked louder at the bird
Who was shell shocked by the bard
And squawking louder retreated to the blue.

Note: This poem was written to the prompt, "When Driftwood Ashore was stalked by an unknown bird." Driftwood Ashore is the pseudonym of the poet Shyam Sunder Sharma.

Let Go of Your Anger

Daddy, you might not see
but you are always angry.
I saw this movie where the waves tower
and the ships overpower.
Towards the shore, the ships are washed.
But alas! On the rocks, they are dashed.

Your anger is like those violent waves
that consigns our family to watery graves.
Like jagged rocks lying treacherously in wait,
your anger seals our fate.
Crashed violently against the rocks to pieces.
ripped asunder is the fragile boat of fun and peace.

You say things that are mean,
afterwards, you say you did not mean
what you said
but at that time, it was like a hard slap to the head.
Saying sorry after the anger drains
doesn't set things right again.

I have come to fear you
and shrink in fear from you
when you call
'cause I don't know when into anger you may fall.
You say you don't slap me
but worse than that, I am hurt, Daddy.

I cry for ages
after you fly into rages.
I want to run away
far, far away...
Why Daddy did you bring me into this world
if you cannot with love cherish me in your hold.

I saw my friend with his daddy...
He is his best buddy.
Together they play
and go to the cafe.
I also want to feel loved and safe
not as though, from you I always want to escape.

Daddy, can you do that for me?
Let your anger go free...
Set it afloat in the ocean
And never let it play with our emotions.
If you love me, Daddy
Can you do that for me?

Note: This poem was written to the prompt, "A five-year-old giving his father a lecture on anger management" given on 19 April 2024.

A Diamond in an Ordinary World

Sometimes I feel like I have entered a blackhole
So dark is everything around me.
I seem to have slipped beyond the event horizon,
With the recent turn of events.
And entered a void...
Darkness, emptiness, nothingness.

But there is no lightness to this emptiness
On the contrary, I'm filled with heaviness
And seem to be sucked by a vacuum into the darkness
Where I don't see the light anymore
Constantly warped by space and time.

Speeding towards singularity
I float in the cosmic eye
When singes upon my consciousness a bright star.
"Twinkle, twinkle little star
I wonder what you are
Up above the world so high
Like a diamond in the sky."

It was a woman
Who sat framed by a window wooden.
Around her, I could see a halo
Akin to the full moon's glow.
She was the one who never married
And yet in her arms hundreds of children carried.

Orphans, they were... left at her door
Into whom her life spirit she did pour.
Feeding them, bathing them, educating them,
And today they stand like giant elms...
Smiling, happy, and independent.

For giving happy lives
To those who started life in sadness
For empowering those
Who started life in weakness
She wears the crown of diamonds
And twinkles like a diamond
In a world of ordinary men and women.

Note: This poem was written to the prompt, "Write a piece that contains 3 lines from nursery rhymes" given on 22 April 2024.

The Cacophony of Silence

I went to an old age home and I met people abandoned... Abandoned by their children to silence. Shut out of their lives forever to live in the cacophony of silence. Children who no longer call their parents, no longer find out how they are, and no longer give any love or affection to their old parents. As I hear their stories, I am numbed by the callousness. Numbed into silence with no empty words to offer as platitudes for I could see the finality of acceptance on their faces. My mind raged in the silence.

I railed against what had come of my nation. This, then was my India where parents are worshipped. The India of *atithi devo bhavo*, where even a guest is respected and welcomed into the home. The India where Lord Ganesh circumambulated his parents because that was akin to circumnavigating the universe. In a country where culturally parents were considered to be the Universe, where did this universe break down and they be relegated to the streets like yesterday's rubbish?

A tailor who after an accident had lost his ability to earn and his treatment demanded money. A man who had taken voluntary retirement and made the mistake of turning his savings to his children. Was a man's worth only as good as his money? And, this disease was not restricted to a section of society but spread like the bubonic plague. As I heard the story of children buying more cars, and adding rooms to houses...the questions hung in the air. Oh! Why was there no room in the heart for aging parents? Where had society disintegrated?

No words of consolation come as an old woman lost to dementia sits on a chair by the gate and waits for her son, a son who has not visited her once in 20 years.

I meet a paralysed lady who can't talk and has been relegated to the din of her own mind. She was living on the streets...abandoned by children... unbathed and insects had made a home in her matted hair. Neither could she talk nor I. Just the silence throbbed. It raged like a storm with unanswered questions. It crashed over us like a tempest for now the tears had long since dried. Tired after a lifetime of caring, did they not deserve to be cared for in their second childhood? Who if not their children would do that? Thrown out of the house because their motor functions were weakening...the spoon took long to connect with the mouth and the food dribbled on the clothes. Ha! What a bucket of rubbish is that!

The silence throbs all around. The air sits heavy with the silence of impotent fate. There is no pitter-patter of tiny feet, no shouts of joy but only tears of tribulation in the heavy silence. There is nothing to relieve the tedium from the cacophony of the silence of one's mind. The air also shouts why them?

As another's diapers are changed by strangers living on benevolence of others I am struck by the dissonance in society. Those who have parents abandon them for money, and those who don't have the money accept them. But these are only a handful. The majority is relegated to silence... silence from children, from society, from caregivers. And the silence cries, begs to be broken, for hearts to be mended, for the aged to be cared for.

Note: This piece was written to the prompt, “The cacophony of silence” given on 23 April 2024.

Fighting Like Kids

They were old and sat calmly together,
shelling peas in sultry conversation,
when piped a complaint about another.
"She sits by the gate for her relation.
Why did she sit down in my location?"
An open war broke out between the two.
In angry voices, they fought like kids true,
till the caretakers downed the hysteria.
And shortly, forgotten was the issue
for the real issue was dementia.

Note: This piece was written to the prompt, "Two adults fighting like children" given on 26 April 2024 for Pandorathon 2024. The poem is a dizain, which is a traditional form made up of just one ten-line stanza, with each line having ten syllables (that's an even hundred in total). The rhyme scheme for a dizain is ABABBCCDCD.

Afterword

By Gayatri Majumdar

"In the temple of dawn,

light, my spirits adorn." (*The Call of Light*) – Avantika Singh

I consider it serendipitous to have met Avantika last year at a poetry festival hosted in Auroville, Tamil Nadu, India. Over the three days or so, we quite naturally gravitated towards each other, engaging in long conversations close to our hearts. I could sense her righteousness and deep commitment to the causes behind her beaming smile. I was then eager to go over her poems for this Afterword.

It is in these poems I found a person who, despite (or because of) the trials and tribulations life dealt (I'm convinced there were many), is deeply spiritual and whose lifelong effort has been to transcend the prosaic, connecting intimately with the cosmos and nature. Deeply compassionate, her endeavor has been to uplift humanity through her work and spread the message of peace by 'Melt(ing) away the barriers'. I live in Pondicherry (next to Sri Aurobindo Ashram and Auroville), both of which the Mother (Mirra Alfassa) had a hand in establishing, the reason I found meeting the poet a serendipitous occurrence. There is a strong belief in her that there are other ways of living, of being, of belonging other than what we have been accustomed to, or what has conditioned us. The first step to finding that place is aspiration, indeed a quality that is the poet's forte.

Avantika's poems in the first three sections of the book – 'Temple of Twilight', 'Cosmic Dance' and 'Float Free', and even in 'Quilling for Humanity' are replete with beauty and serenity, a sense of connection with nature. Deeply reflective, they are a result of a major shift in her perspective to find the bliss, not just for herself but for the entire humanity.

"Let the sun's rays fall
upon the wavering slopes of my mind
lighting the deep crevices within
where dwell darkness, despair, and doubt.
Let them dispel the tenebrosity and turmoil,
awakening my mind to the light
of changeless consciousness
where flowers of hope bloom." – *An Invocation to Sunrise*

And,

"Melt away the barriers of the mind,
for they are just illusions...
and find yourself
lighter…
released from the burden of judgement.
Find yourself floating like
gold dust on sunbeams…
warm sunshine on a winter morning." – *Melt Away the Boundaries*

She often laments at what we have done to ourselves and become, constantly craving to satisfy our materialistic desires to fill the void inside leaving behind a trail of disasters and broken lives, destroying our environment almost beyond repair. In *The Cacophony of Silence*, she laments, "I went to an old age home and I met people abandoned... Abandoned by their children to silence. Shut out of their lives forever to live in the cacophony of silence. Children who no longer call their parents, no longer find out how they are, and no longer give any love or affection to their old parents. As I hear their stories, I am numbed by the callousness. Numbed into silence with no empty words to offer as platitudes, for I could see the finality of acceptance on their faces."

Avantika is willing to explore any available avenue to connect with others (many poems in the book are a result of various prompts on Facebook) to drive home the point. With a certain humility, she writes poems about other poets/writers she admires, which is rare (in another world).

"Today, the roads are a mess
With branded cars vrooming to impress.
Sadly, these youngsters of today
Will only know speed and luxurious display
And not the camaraderie born of humbleness
With a life led with some purpose." – *Letting off Steam*

And

"In the crowded bazaar of life,
we often forget our minutia...
how like a speck of dust we are
in the universe's largeness.
Then why the ego and the fights?
Why the gory wars and bloodshed?
Let the dust of our existence
Add to the energy of life." – *The Orange Glow*

In her deep subconscious, the poet is aware that the peace has to be first found within; once it's established, one easily becomes the gold dust in sunbeams sans ego, an instrument of the Divine, which leads us by our hands. That is why Avantika's poems that overflow with enchanting imagery are so inspirational, giving us enormous hope that all is not lost.

Avantika dedicates an entire section in the book to women – 'Being Women' with some outstanding poems in it. In *She – I*, she keenly observes,

"I was most taken
by a painting of Leonid Afremov unmistaken...
The painting of a flamenco dancer,
who conveyed the romance of life within her.

Swirls of oil on canvas
made up the ruffles of her dress,
symbolising the colours of a woman's life
by the strokes of the knife."

Some poems, added later to the volume in the section 'Temple of Twilight' are steeped in devotion, mindfulness and strong imagery, particularly in poems such as 'Sunrise in Kashi' and 'A Sunset in the Sundarbans'. In 'A Morning at Shankracharya Temple' she writes,

"a crossway of sorts,
a confluence in time of thoughts
for here did Shankracharya*ji* meditate
and carried forth the word of the Advait,
and to these harmonies, the air still vibrates...
a cosmic crossing, the *brahman* merging...
... and I becoming...
Aham Brahmasmi..."

The poem "Is Pinkness a thing" enthrals, written in response to a prompt. Here, the poet is fearless, beginning to question the staple that has been fed to us debasing our strengths and our capabilities over the centuries.

"When did I come to be associated with gender?
Was it when I was blushing tender?
When did I become a social construct?
A woman is nature's greatest strength,
not one colour, but an amalgamation of all in her depth.

Is the extended celebration of pink
An exploitation to hear the monies clink?
A stereotyping that needs to be broken?" – *Is Pinkness a thing?*

May the book find all those who share her passion for ending all manners of sufferings on this blue planet we call home, and those who want to read Avantika's absolutely remarkable revelatory poems.

Gayatri Majumdar

Poet, Publisher, Editor

14 March 2025

Gayatri Majumdar founded, edited and published the critically acclaimed Indian literary journal, *The Brown Critique* (since 1995) which featured hundreds of Indian and international poets. Her seven books include four volumes of poems including the recent one longlisted for The Wise Owl Poetry Award, 2025 – *A warm place with no memory* (Red River, India).

Gayatri is the Festival Director of the popular annual Pondicherry/Auroville Poetry Festival. Her poems and articles on travel and spirituality have been published widely in Indian and international journals and anthologies. Earlier in 2025, her work was included in *Words' Waltz, Selected Poems of Twenty-One Contemporary Indian Poets*. While Hindi translations of her poems by Rekha Sehti will be a part of the anthology, *Jugalbandi – Angrezhi ki Samakalin Stri Kavita*.

She currently lives in Pondicherry where she is associated with Sri Aurobindo Society, handling its publications work and she edits the poetry page of *Sri Aurobindo's Action Journal*.

Critical Review

Like the million rays of a dazzling sun, perennially shining, poetry never sets in the horizon of Avantika Vijay Singh's resplendent mind. She becomes the centre in a space and dimension that launches a myriad thoughts asunder, illuminating the real, the spiritual, the ephemeral and the eternal, as she traverses across latitudes and longitudes of her Motherland, touching the cardinal points in a way only she could.

The adoration and reverence with which the poet paraphrases her devotion to the Divine in Existence, makes her a true "Child of the Earth". In this shimmering thought field, she brings to the spotlight womanhood, as colourful as a perfect rainbow, wherein hues flutter with triumph as she recalls the special women in her life. Her empathy and love for humanity surfaces like dappled moonlit waters of care and concern for the downtrodden, sensitive to the sufferings of the less fortunate souls.

Her understanding of science as a religion by itself shines like a beacon of Vedanta where she sees All as One and One as All as a Super Consciousness merging the Macro and the Micro, in the enigma of multifarious Truths. One cannot but stay awestruck as one reads Avantika's verses that take the reader on an Odyssey of introspection and realisation, so aesthetically portrayed in the lyricism of her poetry. "Gold Dust on Sunbeams" alights right outside the vision of the reader, bringing to light that life itself is a celebration.

Geethanjali Dilip

Poet, Curator—Yercaud Poetry Festival (YPF), Professor of French